DRIVING SKILLS

D1450468

THE
MOTORCYCLING
MANUAL

London: HMSO

Developed and prepared by COMIND

Design and writing: Nick Lynch
Illustrations: Vicky Squires
Photography: Unit 18 Photography, Norwich

© Crown copyright 1991
First published 1991
ISBN 011 550974 7

Acknowledgements

HMSO and DSA are grateful for the help and support given by

- Revetts (Motorcycle Dealers) of Ipswich, who supplied the motorcycles photographed in this book, and

- Cambridgeshire Constabulary, Hallens Motorcycles and Cambridge Tyre Service

"Safe Riding for Life"

Motorcycling can be a pleasant and exhilarating experience, as well as an economic means of transport.

However, the volume of traffic and faster, more powerful motorcycles, more than ever before make it essential for riders to expect the unexpected and question the actions of other road users. After all, it's in *your* interest to make safety *your* responsibility!

The Driving Standards Agency (DSA) is an Agency of the Department of Transport. Its primary aim is to promote road safety in Great Britain through the advancement of driving standards. This manual is designed to help motorcyclists at all levels of experience to master safe riding as a life skill.

Whether you're an experienced motorcyclist or a new rider, you'll realise that riding not only requires skill in handling your machine but also the ability to 'read' the road. Good observation and anticipation are essential to safe riding.

The manual is a step-by-step guide to motorcycling, covering all aspects: from choosing your machines and the correct protective clothing to defensive riding and the importance of proper training. It's an essential reference book for all motorcyclists, however experienced — and instructors too. Read it carefully, and put into practice the advice it gives.

Above all, make sure *your* aim is *"Safe Riding for Life"*

Keith Cameron
Chief Driving Examiner
Driving Standards Agency

Contents

Riding a motorcycle is a responsible business.

Compared with driving other road vehicles, riding a motorcycle puts you at greater risk from other road users. If you're involved in an accident, the chances of injuring yourself are **very** high.

The machine, the 'gear', the road, the weather, and the traffic, are all part of the environment that you have to live in when you're riding a motorcycle.

How well you get on depends on you.

This section covers the psychological and mental attitude of the rider and the demands of safe motorcycling.

1. The Rider

Your attitude

People take up motorcycling for many different reasons.

Some take it up as a cheap form of transport and have no interest in the exhilarating, sporting, fashionable or cult elements.

To others it is an exciting recreation. To yet others it is a sport. To another group it is a way of life.

Motorcycling can and does meet the needs of all these groups, and the vast majority of motorcyclists are responsible and sensible.

They have a positive attitude to motorcycling.

Fig. 1.1

Other road users

Experienced motorcyclists probably take much more notice of other road users than any other group on the road.

They do this partly out of a sense of self preservation, in the knowledge that they have no protective shell to take the impact if they get it wrong.

Unfortunately, motorcycling has a hard way of teaching those who fail to learn from the advice and example of others.

Motorcyclists also take notice because their vulnerability tends to make them more sensitive to the needs of others.

Reacting to bad driving

Try not to react emotionally if another road user does something wrong. The strains of riding can often cause riders to overreact.

Don't try to teach a bad driver a lesson. It's not your job, and it could involve you in an accident. Anyway, it would probably be a waste of time.

The benefits of good technique

Master the techniques set out in this manual. They were developed by experienced riders, and they make sense.

Others will learn from watching you. They'll appreciate your courtesy and good riding.

A safe attitude

Motorcycling can be very exhilarating, but you must not go beyond the bounds of caution.

Putting yourself at risk is foolish. Don't do it on public roads.

If you have an accident, you'll almost certainly involve others on today's roads.

Develop a safe attitude from the very beginning. Study the Highway Code and think 'safety'.

That way you'll enjoy your riding a lot longer.

1. The Rider

Concentration

Concentration is survival. Riding on today's roads demands full concentration.

Concentration means keeping your mind on the job and excluding everything else. One lapse can mean disaster.

If you're driving a car, a small lapse in concentration might result in some expensive bodywork damage, but not nearly so expensive as the damage to human bodywork which results even from some low-speed motorcycle accidents.

Many factors can disrupt your concentration.

Personal matters

Leave your emotions behind when you ride.

If something upsets or worries you, think twice before starting a journey. Better still, use some other means of transport.

Personal feelings and concentration don't mix.

If something upsets you on the road, never give vent to your anger or frustration by riding very fast or by behaving discourteously to other road users.

Health

Health is one personal matter which can disrupt your concentration.

A bad cold can not only distract your mind, it can also slow your reaction.

Stay off your motorcycle if you feel ill in any way.

A fit rider is also more alert than one who is unfit. So take suitable exercise.

Proper clothing

Something else which does not aid concentration is cold or wet weather.

Cold hands, cold feet, or being cold or wet all over, is a guarantee that your concentration will be reduced.

Your reactions will also be slower.

Alcohol

Alcohol will reduce your ability to ride safely. It's an offence to ride a motorcycle or a moped if you have in your blood more than 80 milligrams of alcohol per 100 millilitres of blood.

Be safe: don't drink **at all** when you ride.

Drugs

Taking some drugs is a criminal offence. Riding when you're under their influence is unforgivable and can be fatal.

Warning - invalid insurance

Riding under the influence of alcohol or drugs could invalidate your insurance.

Prescribed medicines

If your doctor prescribes medicines for you, ask if your riding will be affected. Some over-the-counter medicines can have a harmful effect on riding.

Remember, the responsibility is yours. Read the label, or ask the chemist or your doctor.

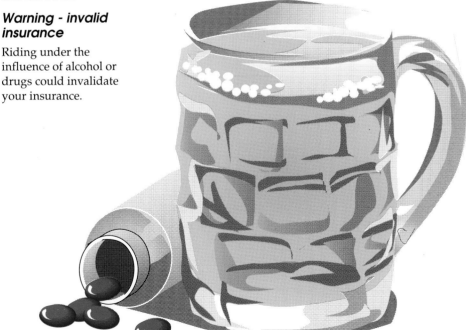

Fig. 1.2

1. The Rider

Economy

'A cheap form of transport.'

Yes! Motorcycling is economical, but safety must never be sacrificed for economy.

Cutting costs down until you are below the minimum level of safety is not a very wise course of action.

If you're a beginner, you must accept that motorcycling has considerable costs.

Be sure you can afford to start at the level of entry you're aiming for, whether it's commuting to work on a moped or taking two-hundred-mile weekend trips. Running some models is more expensive than running some types of car.

You'll have to consider

- The purchase price of the motorcycle
- The on-the-road costs: Vehicle Excise Duty and insurance
- The running costs: fuel, maintenance and so on
- The cost of adequate clothing
- The cost of training. All riders must take proper training.

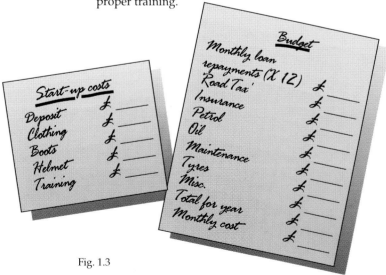

Fig. 1.3

2. The Motorcyclist and the Law

Owning and riding a motorcycle carries with it legal requirements.

You must satisfy some of these before you begin to ride on the public road. Others apply after you start to ride.

Most of these requirements are there to protect you and other road users. If you neglect them, you and your family could be the first losers.

Complying with the law is not cheap. It can cost as much as the motorcycle itself.

Failing to comply could turn out much more expensive.

Motorcycle Riders

To ride a motorcycle on the public road, you must

- Be at least 17 years of age
- Have a driving licence which specifies you are entitled to ride motorcycles (Category A - formerly Group D)

That licence can be any of the following

1. Full Motorcycle Licence
2. Provisional Motorcycle Licence*
3. Full Car or Moped Licence. These automatically give provisional motorcycle entitlement*
4. A Provisional Driving Licence with provisional motorcycle entitlement*

* If you hold one of these licences, see Compulsory Basic Training and Provisional Motorcycle Entitlement on this page.

Compulsory Basic Training (CBT)

Before you are allowed to ride on the road unaccompanied, you must attend a CBT course, if

- The provisional motorcycle entitlement of your licence started on or after 1st December 1990, and
- You do not hold a valid Part 1 Test Certificate

When you have reached a satisfactory standard, you will be issued with a Certificate of Completion (DL 196).

You are allowed to ride on the road without taking a CBT course, if

- You hold a licence with provisional motorcycle entitlement which started before 1st December 1990
- You hold a valid Part 1 Test Certificate

However, you must have a DL 196 certificate or a valid Part 1 Test Certificate before you can take the Motorcycle Test.

Figure 2.1 opposite gives more detailed information on how CBT affects learner motorcyclists.

See Section 6 for details of what comprises a CBT course.

Provisional Motorcycle Entitlement

This entitles learners to ride a machine of up to 125cc or a maximum power output of 9kW.

You must not

- Ride on motorways
- Carry a pillion passenger
- Ride without L-plates

Two-year limit

A Provisional Motorcycle Licence is valid for two years only. You must take and pass the Motorcycle Test within two years, or you'll have to wait a year before you can apply for another provisional licence.

This restriction does not apply if your provisional motorcycle entitlement from age 17 is granted by a full car or moped licence.

Fig. 2.1 Compulsory Basic Training for Learner Motorcyclists

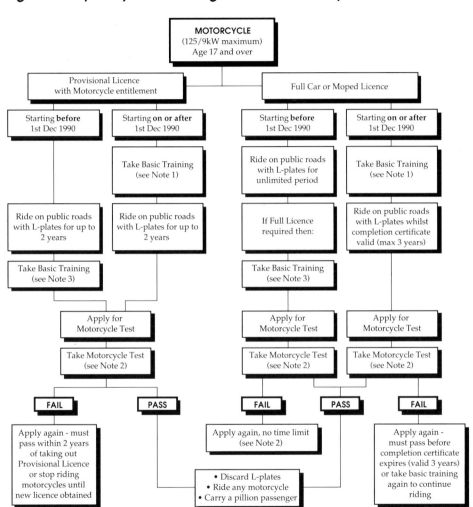

Note 1: If your licence started on or after 1 Dec 1990, you do not have to take CBT if you
(a) live and ride on specified off-shore islands, or   (b) hold a valid Certificate of Completion (DL196) obtained during previous motorcycle entitlement or when riding a moped, or   (c) hold a valid Part 1 Test certificate (valid 5 years).
Note 2: If you wish to take a motorcycle test on a solo machine, you will need either a valid Part 1 Test Certificate or a Certificate of Completion (DL196). From 1 June 1991, you will need a Certificate of Completion (DL196) if you want to take your test on a motorcycle fitted with a sidecar.
Note 3: If you have passed a Part 1 Test and still hold a valid Part 1 Test Certificate (valid 5 years), you can apply to take the Motorcycle Test without having to take CBT.

Moped Riders

To ride a moped on the public road, you must

- Be at least 16 years of age
- Have a driving licence which specifies you are entitled to ride mopeds (category P-formerly Group E)

That licence can be any of the following

Aged 16 but under 17

1. Full Moped Licence
2. Provisional Moped Licence*

Aged 17 and over

As 1 and 2 above, but also

3. Full Car or Motorcycle Licence
4. A Provisional Driving Licence with moped entitlement*

 * If you hold one of these licences, see Compulsory Basic Training and Provisional Moped Entitlement on this page.

Compulsory Basic Training (CBT)

If your Provisional Moped Entitlement started on or after 1st December 1990, you must attend a CBT course before you are allowed to ride on the road unaccompanied.

When you have reached a satisfactory standard, you will be issued with a Certificate of Completion (DL 196).

If your Provisional Moped Entitlement started before 1st December 1990, you are allowed to ride on the road unaccompanied, without having to take a CBT course. However, you must have a DL196 certificate before you can take a Moped test.

Figure 2.2 opposite gives more detailed information about how CBT affects learner moped riders.

See Section 6 for details of what comprises a CBT course.

NOTE: If you obtain a Certificate of Completion on a moped, you can use it to ride a 125cc/9kW motorcycle with L-plates, provided you are 17 or over.

Provisional Moped Entitlement

This only entitles you to ride a machine of up to 50cc with a maximum design speed not exceeding 30 mph.

You must not

- Ride on motorways
- Carry a pillion passenger
- Ride without L-plates

NOTE: The Provisional Moped Licence is not subject to the same two year limit as the Provisional Motorcycle Licence.

Fig. 2.2 Compulsory Basic Training for Learner Moped Riders

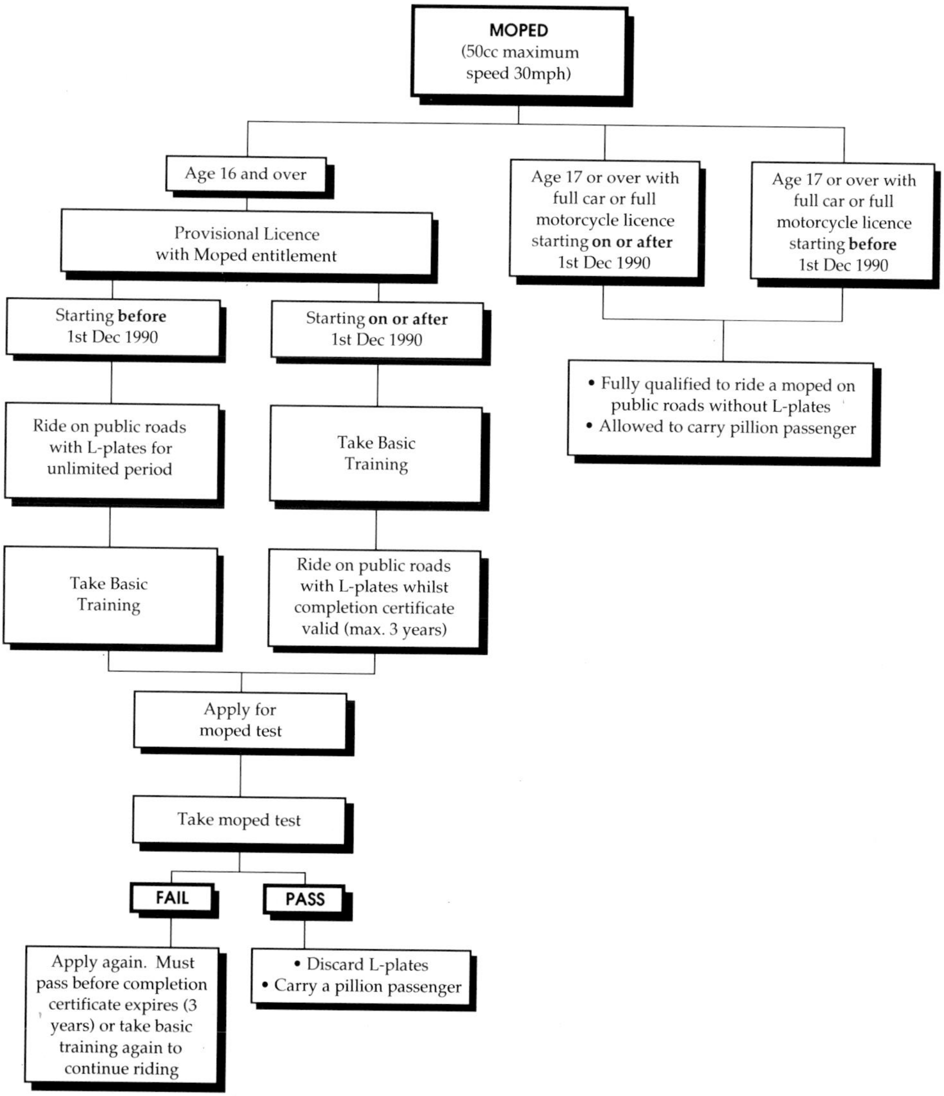

```
                        ┌─────────────────────┐
                        │        MOPED        │
                        │   (50cc maximum     │
                        │    speed 30mph)     │
                        └─────────────────────┘
```

MOPED (50cc maximum speed 30mph)

Age 16 and over

Provisional Licence with Moped entitlement

Starting **before** 1st Dec 1990

Starting **on or after** 1st Dec 1990

Ride on public roads with L-plates for unlimited period

Take Basic Training

Take Basic Training

Ride on public roads with L-plates whilst completion certificate valid (max. 3 years)

Apply for moped test

Take moped test

FAIL

PASS

Apply again. Must pass before completion certificate expires (3 years) or take basic training again to continue riding

• Discard L-plates
• Carry a pillion passenger

Age 17 or over with full car or full motorcycle licence starting **on or after** 1st Dec 1990

Age 17 or over with full car or full motorcycle licence starting **before** 1st Dec 1990

• Fully qualified to ride a moped on public roads without L-plates
• Allowed to carry pillion passenger

The Highway Code

To pass your Motorcycle or Moped Test, you must show a thorough knowledge of the Highway Code, and in everyday riding you should follow the rules set down in it.

Although the Highway Code is not a legal document, the police often use it in court to support their prosecution cases.

Look at the Highway Code as an aid to safe riding.

Don't look at it as a restriction.

Fig 2.3   The Highway Code

The Vehicle Registration Document

This contains details of your motorcycle, make and model, including year of first registration, engine size and number.

It also gives your name and address.

If you buy new

Your dealer will see that you get one of these documents.

If you buy second-hand

Fill in the change of ownership section and send it off to the DVLA at the address given on the document.

You should do this immediately as it is an offence not to notify the DVLA at Swansea.

Vehicle Excise Duty

This is often called 'road tax' or 'vehicle licence'. The owners or the operators of all road vehicles must pay it and display the required disc on the vehicle.

Application form

You can get the Vehicle Licence Application Form at any post office.

Applying

Most main post offices can accept your application, take your money and give you a 'tax disc'.

Or you can send the completed application to the DVLA at the address given on the form.

The Vehicle Excise Duty fee

This varies with engine capacity. The classes are
Up to 150cc
151-250cc
Over 250cc, including three-wheelers

Documents you must present

When you apply to renew your Vehicle Excise Licence ('tax disc'), you must produce two other current documents

- A Vehicle Test Certificate (MOT) if your motorcycle is more than 3 years old
- A valid certificate of insurance

2. The Motorcyclist and the Law

Insurance

It takes a very irresponsible person to ride without insurance. It is illegal, and, should you cause injury to anyone or damage to property, it could be expensive.

Before you take the motorcycle on the public road, get proper insurance cover.

You can arrange this with

- The manufacturer (sometimes)
- The insurance company directly
- A broker
- A motorcycle dealer

Insuring with the insurance company

Direct insurance is probably a little cheaper than the same policy through a broker, but finding the best deal can be time consuming.

Insuring through a broker

A good broker will shop around and find the best policy for you.

Many brokers are linked by computer to the main insurance companies, and will get you comparative quotes very quickly.

Ask around for the name of a reliable broker, don't just walk in off the street.

If you already have car insurance, ask your present insurer first.

Insuring through a motorcycle dealer

A dealer can have direct relations with an insurance company, or arrange insurance through the manufacturer. A dealer might also act as, or work on behalf of, a broker.

Insuring through the manufacturer

Some of the larger manufacturers make arrangements with major insurance companies.

This benefits the motorcyclist by assuring competitive rates.

If you buy new, your dealer will tell you about this.

Types of insurance

Third Party

The legal minimum and the cheapest insurance cover.

The third party is any person you might injure or property you might

damage. You are not covered for damage to your motorcycle or injury to yourself.

If you make a mistake when riding and damage a car, the owner could claim against you.

On the other hand, if someone damaged your motorcycle, you could claim against them.

Third party fire and theft

The same as third party, except that it also covers you against your motorcycle being stolen or damaged by fire.

Comprehensive

The best, but the most expensive.

Apart from covering other persons and property from injury and damage, this covers

- Damage to your machine by unknown persons
- Replacement of parts damaged in an accident
- Personal injury to yourself

Pillion passenger insurance

All policies include compulsory cover of a pillion passenger — regardless of whether you are legally allowed to carry a passenger.

Compensation for a pillion passenger injured in an accident can reach hundreds of thousands of pounds.

The cost of insurance

This varies with
- Your age. The younger you are the more it will cost you
- The make of your motorcycle
- The power and capacity of the engine
- Where you live

Typical engine size groups are
> Up to 100cc
> 101-225cc
> 226-350cc
> 351-600cc
> 601-900cc
> Over 900cc

But this can vary from one insurer to another.

What's insured

This also varies from company to company. Read the small print and ask your insurer or broker. Otherwise you might get a shock when you claim.

You will often have to pay the first £50 or £100 of the cost yourself — this is called the 'excess'.

Buy the best policy you can afford. It could be the cheapest in the end.

CERTIFICATE OF MOTOR INSURANCE 3

1. Description of Vehicles.
Any motor cycle owned by the Policyholder or hired to him under a hire purchase agreement

Certificate No. M.V.C. 009/1234567/09/11

2. Name of Policyholder.
J Smith

3. Effective date of the Commencement of Insurance for the purposes of the relevant Law.
10 Nov 1990

4. Date of Expiry of Insurance.
9 Nov 1991

5. Persons or Classes of Persons entitled to drive.
Those specified by Clause(s)   A   provided that the person driving holds a licence to drive the vehicle or has held and is not disqualified for holding or obtaining such a licence.

A. The Policyholder. The Policyholder may also drive any motor cycle not belonging to him and not hired to him under a hire purchase agreement.

B. The Policyholder. The Policyholder may also drive any motor cycle not belonging to him and not hired to him under a hire purchase agreement provided that this extension shall not apply in respect of any motor cycle:
(a) the property of or in the custody of or company of motor traders of which the Policyholder is a partner director or employee
(b) which is in the custody or control of the Policyholder in the course of his business as a motor trader.

C. The Policyholder.

D. Any person who is driving on the order or with the permission of the Policyholder provided the vehicle is not hired to such person.

E.

provided the vehicle is not hired to such person.

6. Limitations as to use.
As defined by Clause   F

F. Business social domestic and pleasure excluding racing pacemaking speedtesting or the carriage of passengers for hire or reward.

G. Business social domestic and pleasure excluding racing pacemaking speedtesting the carriage of passengers for hire or reward or use of any motor cycle unless a sidecar is permanently attached thereto.

H. Social domestic pleasure and by the Policyholder in person in connection with his business excluding hiring racing pacemaking or speedtesting.

I hereby certify that the policy to which this Certificate relates satisfies the requirements of the relevant Law applicable in Great Britain, Northern Ireland, the Isle of Man, the Island of Guernsey, the Island of Jersey and the Island of Alderney.

Authorised Insurers

Head Office:
Pitheavlis, Perth, Scotland PH2 0NH

Chief General Manager.

NOTE: For full details of the insurance cover reference should be made to the policy.

ADVICE TO THIRD PARTIES: Nothing contained in this Certificate affects your right as a Third Party to make a claim.

This certificate evidences minimum statutory (i.e. Third Party) cover only.

WARNING For change of vehicle, transfer of interest or termination of insurance — SEE OVER.

Fig. 2.4   Certificate of insurance

2. The Motorcyclist and the Law

The Certificate of insurance

A short and simple document which certifies

- Who is insured
- The types of vehicle covered
- The kind of insurance cover
- The period of cover
- The main conditions

Sometimes a broker will give you a temporary certificate or 'cover note' while you're waiting for the real thing.

Keep the certificate safe and produce it

- If the police ask you
- When you apply to renew your Vehicle Excise Licence

The policy document

This contains the full details of the contract between you and the insurance company.

It's written in small print, and usually in legal language — although some companies have simplified their policies.

If you don't understand anything ask your broker or the insurance company to explain.

Accidents

If you're involved in an accident you must stop and give, to anyone having cause to ask for them,

- Your name and address, the owner's name and address, and the registration number of the vehicle. If you are unable to do so, you must report the accident to the police within 24 hours.
- The name and address of your insurer

This applies no matter how minor, or whose fault, the accident was.

You must call the police if any person is injured, however slightly

The Vehicle Test Certificate

The so-called MOT test applies to all motorcycles, mopeds, and scooters three years old and over.

The test must be done every year by a Vehicle Testing Station appointed by the Vehicle Inspectorate, an executive agency of the Department of Transport.

These testing stations are inspected regularly.

Vehicles which must be tested

If your bike is more than three years old, you must have a current MOT Test Certificate.

You will not be able to renew your Vehicle Excise Licence without this.

Testing time

You can have your motorcycle tested as much as one month before

- Your motorcycle reaches its third year
- The current certificate runs out. The expiry date of the new certificate will be one year after the expiry date of the old one

Failure

If your motorcycle fails, you must

- Have the repairs done
- Have the motorcycle re-tested

Fees

Ask your Vehicle Testing Station about the current test and re-test fees.

Purpose of the test

The purpose of the test is to see if your machine is mechanically safe to ride on the public road.

It is not a guarantee that your machine is mechanically safe at any point during the life of the certificate.

Just because you have a current certificate, don't assume that your motorcycle is

- Completely legal. The certificate might be about to expire. Since the test, your tyres might have worn below the legal limit, for example
- Completely safe to ride

You must not ride your motorcycle on the road without a valid test certificate unless

- You are taking it to an MOT testing station for a test, by prior arrangement, or taking it away from the station
- You are taking it to have corrected the defects for which the bike failed

What kind of motorcycle do you need?

Motorcycles come in many different types and sizes.

Each type has different features. Some will suit your needs, others will not.

Before you buy, think carefully about what you want from the motorcycle.

Otherwise you could end up buying a bike which doesn't suit your needs.

Only part of the process

Buying the motorcycle is only part of the process of getting on the road and riding safely. You must also think about the costs of

- Insurance and Vehicle Excise Duty
- Special clothing
- Running and maintenance costs

This section describes the various types of motorcycle and their main features. While some may fall into more than one category, the main types are explained here.

3. Choosing a Motorcycle

Mopeds

Machines under 50cc engine capacity which are not designed for speeds of more than 30mph.

If you hold a Full Car or Motorcycle Driving Licence, you can ride a moped without L-plates.

Fig 3.1 Moped

Learner motorcycles

Suitable for learners.

Features

- Engine up to 125cc
- Power output not exceeding 9kW (about 12 bhp)
- Easy to ride and maintain

Fig. 3.2 Learner motorcycle

Commuter motorcycles

Although any kind of motorcycle can be used to take you to and from work, these are ideal for short trips, and for heavy traffic in towns.

Features

- 50-250cc engine capacity
- Economical to buy and run
- Easy to ride and maintain

You need a Full Motorcycle Licence to ride a machine over 125cc.

Fig 3.3   Commuter motorcycle

Sports motorcycles

Suitable for longer distance riding at higher speeds.

Features

- Racing styling
- Large engine capacity (250-1300cc)
- Capable of very high speeds (up to 160 mph: far above the legal speed limit in the United Kingdom and most EC countries)
- Expensive to maintain and run

Not only do you need a Full Motorcycle Licence to ride one of these, you also need a lot of experience.

Fig. 3.4   Sports motorcycle

3. Choosing a Motorcycle

Touring motorcycles

Suitable for leisurely, long-distance riding.

Features

- Large engine (500 to 1500cc)
- Lower acceleration
- Lower fuel consumption than sports bikes
- Relaxed riding position
- Very comfortable for long journeys
- Luggage carrying capacity

You need a Full Motorcycle Licence to ride one of these.

Fig. 3.5   Touring motorcycle

Off-Road bikes (trail bikes)

Dual purpose bikes: can be used on and off the road.

Features

- Powerful engines (50 to 1000cc). Capable of up to 100 mph.
- Very tough. Built for rough riding.
- Dual-purpose tyres
- Gear ratios suit both road and off-road riding

Fig. 3.6   Off-road motorcycle

4. Clothing and Weather Protection

Special motorcycling clothing
- Protects you from the weather and from some types of injury
- Helps other road users to see you

This section tells you about
- The different types of clothing
- How you benefit from them
- Different material and their features
- What to wear at different times of the year
- How to buy

This section also covers motorcycle fairings and handlebar muffs, which also protect the rider against the elements.

4. Clothing and Weather Protection

Aids to being seen

In daylight

Fluorescent clothing will
- Help other road users to see you
- Reduce the risk of accident

These include tabards (waistcoat) and belts in fluorescent yellow or orange.

Figure 4.1 shows how these help other road users to see you.

You must be clearly visible from **all** sides.

Fluorescent clothing does <u>not</u> help much in the dark. See page 25.

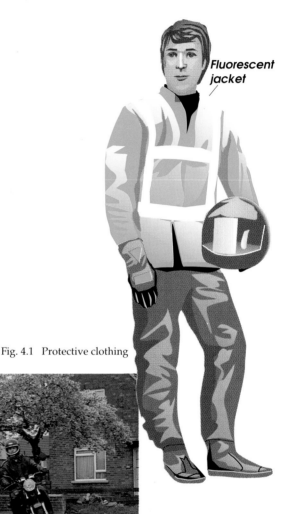

Fluorescent jacket

Fig. 4.1   Protective clothing

Fig. 4.2   Fluorescent clothing is very effective

> **DO!**
> Always wear clothing which ensures you are easily seen.
>
> Use dipped headlamps.

Aids to being seen

In the dark

Reflective belts or patches are a must in the dark. They

- Reflect the headlamps of other vehicles
- Make you much more visible from a long distance in the dark

Reflective strips on the back of your gloves or gauntlets help other road users when you give an arm signal.

You must be clearly visible from **all** sides.

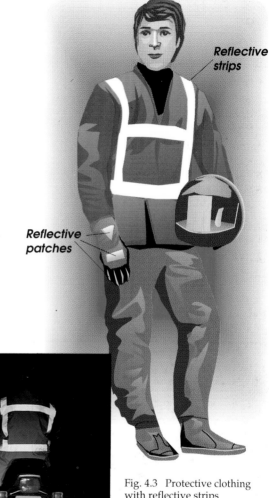

Reflective strips

Reflective patches

Fig. 4.3 Protective clothing with reflective strips

> **DO!**
> Always wear clothing which ensures you are easily seen.

Fig. 4.4 Reflective strips are very effective

4. Clothing and Weather Protection

Protective clothing

Special clothing will protect you
- From the cold and wet
- From some kinds of injury

Protection from the cold and wet

A cold and wet rider cannot concentrate fully on riding safely.

When you're cold you need much more time to react.

If you ride without proper clothing, you're a danger to yourself and to other road users.

Padding

Padding

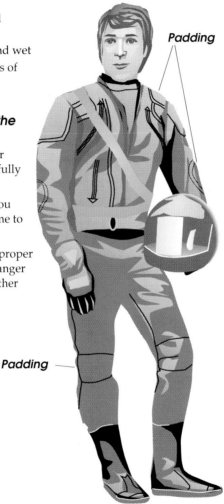

Fig. 4.5 Motorcycle leathers

Leathers

Leathers are special motorcycling outfits. They are not designed to wear over your normal clothes.

Advantages
- Less wind resistance
- More protection from gravel burns if you come off

Disadvantages
- Expensive to buy
- Usually not waterproof, only showerproof. You'll need a nylon oversuit for very wet weather.

You can buy leathers
- Either lined or unlined
- As one- or two-piece suits

When you're buying, look for extra padding at critical points such as elbows and knees.

Beware of 'fashion' leather clothing which will not give the protection of proper motorcycling leathers.

Outer clothing

These fit over your ordinary clothes and must be able to

- Protect you against the elements
- Help keep some kinds of injury to a minimum if you come off

Types

- Two piece: jacket and trousers
- One-piece suits (overall type)
- Lined
- Unlined

Fitting

Outer clothing should be loose enough to allow

- Freedom of movement
- Extra layers underneath in cold weather

Reflective panels

Some suits have built in reflective panels. The more reflectivity you have the easier you will be seen.

Underclothing

Extra layers of underclothing can boost your insulation.

Thermal underwear is light and very warm.

Ordinary 'long johns' are cheaper and also warm.

Materials

Nylon is the most popular material now. Other materials are also available — such as waxed cotton.

Different makes of nylon suits vary in their ability to keep out water. Look for the makes with a 100% waterproof guarantee.

Fig. 4.6 Oversuit

DO!
Buy the best motorcycling clothes you can afford.

DON'T!
- Ride in very bad weather unless you're wearing suitable clothes to keep you warm and dry
- Ride in shorts, no matter how hot the weather

4. Clothing and Weather Protection

Gloves and gauntlets

Cold hands break your concentration and slow down your reaction.

So, good gloves or gauntlets are essential for riding.

These must be able to

- Keep your hands warm
- Allow you to work the controls easily as well
- Protect your hands in an accident

Gauntlets prevent wind and rain from driving up your sleeves. However, the rain can run down your sleeves inside them. Overmitts with elasticated armbands prevent this.

Leather is the most suitable material for gloves. It's tough and supple.

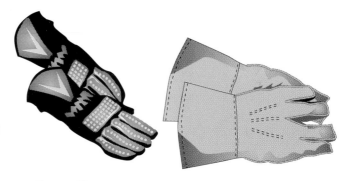

Overmitts

Leather is not always waterproofed. It may be water resistant.

In very wet weather, waterproof overmitts
- Keep your gloves dry
- Give extra protection

Some types have elasticated arm bands to keep the rain from running down your sleeves into your gauntlets.

Fig. 4.7 Gloves, gauntlets and overmitts

Heated gloves

These connect up to the motorcycle and use electricity to heat an element woven into the fabric.

Inner gloves

These give your hands extra protection from cold. Your gloves or gauntlets need to be a little larger.

> **DON'T!**
> Ride bare-handed or bare-armed — even over a short distance. You have no protection in an accident.

Footwear

What applies to gloves also applies to footwear.

Strong boots

- Protect your feet, ankles, and calves from knocks from the footrest or kick-start lever
- Reduce the risk of injury if you have an accident
- Protect your feet from cold and wet

Types of boots

The most suitable material for motorcycle boots is leather.

Leather boots

Leather gives best protection from impact and from the cold.

Lined and unlined

Leather boots can be either lined or unlined.

Rubber boots

These are

- Much cheaper than leather
- Waterproof

They are also available lined or unlined. Leather look boots are also available.

Overboots

Leather is not always waterproofed, so you might need waterproof overboots to protect your leather boots when riding in wet weather.

Extra socks

Boots should be large enough to take an extra pair of socks in cold weather.

Thermal socks are best, but any kind of heavy sock will help.

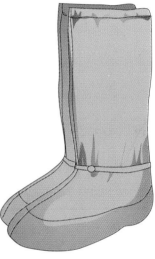

Fig. 4.9   Overboots

Fig. 4.8   Leather boots

> **DO!**
> Buy the best boots you can afford

> **DON'T!**
> Ride in sandals, or trainers — even for a short distance.

4. Clothing and Weather Protection

Safety Helmets

By law, you must wear a safety helmet when riding a motorcycle, unless you are a member of the Sikh religion and wear a turban.

All helmets sold in the United Kingdom must

- Carry a BSI kitemark (see Fig. 4.10)
- Comply with British Standard Number BS 6658

When worn riding, they must also

- Fit properly
- Be fastened

Fig. 4.10   Kitemark

Types of safety helmet

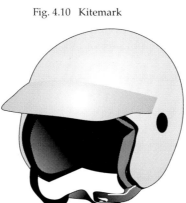

Fig. 4.11   Open-face helmet

Open-face helmets

- Preferred by riders who feel closed in by full-face helmets.
- Can be fitted with a clip-on visor. If not, wear goggles.
- Don't protect the chin in an accident.

Whichever type of helmet you choose, you must make sure that it's properly fastened.

Full-face helmets

- Cover the head fully, and have hinged visors
- Preferred by many riders because they
  - protect the face in an accident
  - offer more weather protection than open-face helmets.

Not only is it illegal to ride in a helmet that isn't fastened, it's unsafe.

Some helmet straps have a velcro fastening as well as a buckle. Make sure the buckle is properly fastened — the velcro alone is not strong enough to keep your helmet on in an accident.

Fig. 4.12   Full face helmet

Safety Helmets

Helmet materials

Glass fibre
- Heavier than polycarbonate
- Lasts longer than polycarbonate
- Easy to clean

Polycarbonate
- Lighter than glass fibre
- Must not be painted or have stickers affixed
- Must not be cleaned with solvents

Kevlar
- An extremely tough material which combines the strength and durability of glass fibre with the lightness of polycarbonate

Damage to helmet

If you damage your helmet even slightly, buy a new one. The slightest damage can make a helmet unreliable.

If your helmet receives any serious impact, but is not obviously damaged, it's safer to buy a new one.

Underhelmets (balaclava type)

These go under your helmet to give you extra warmth.

They're made of silk, cotton or thermal material.

Paint and stickers

Don't
- Paint your helmet
- Put stickers or reflective strips on it

DO!
- Buy a new helmet. You never know what's happened to a second-hand one
- Make sure your helmet fits. Too tight, it could affect your concentration. Too loose, and it could come off in an accident.

DON'T!
- Wear a damaged or repaired helmet
- Ride without a helmet

It's illegal and very dangerous.

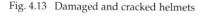

Fig. 4.13   Damaged and cracked helmets

4. Clothing and Weather Protection

Visor or goggles

A visor or a pair of goggles is vital to protect your eyes from wind, rain, insects, and road dirt.

Fig. 4.14 Goggles

The Law on visors and goggles

All visors and goggles must

- Comply with British Standard
  - BS 4110 XA, or
  - BS 4110 YA, or
  - BS 4110 ZA
- Display a Kitemark (Fig. 4.10)

Damaged or scratched goggles.

Don't wear these. They can

- Distort your view
- Cause dazzle from the sun or from lights of oncoming vehicles

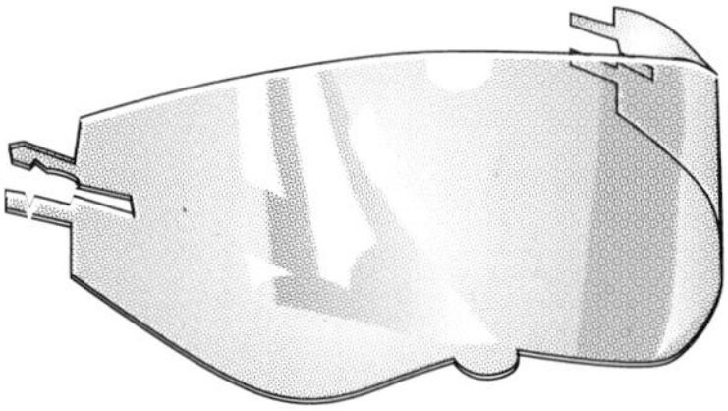

Fig. 4.15 Visor

Fig. 4.16 Glare from lights of oncoming traffic through a scratched goggle/visor

Wearing glasses

If you normally wear glasses, you must by law wear them when you ride.

Tinted glasses, visors or goggles

Don't wear these in the dark or in poor light.

Cleaning your visor or goggles

Keep them as clean as possible to give you a clear view of the road ahead.

You may need to stop if your visor or goggles need cleaning during your journey.

Wash them in warm soapy water.

DON'T!

- Use solvents or petrol to clean your visor or goggles.
- Wipe your goggles or visor with your glove, unless they are scratch resistant or your glove has a stitched-in wiper.

Some goggles and visors scratch very easily.

Motorcycle fairings

Touring fairings

These protect the hands, legs and feet from the wind and rain.

Fig. 4.17   Touring fairing

Sports fairings

These give some protection, but they are mainly intended to cut wind resistance.

Fig. 4.18   Sports fairing

Handlebar fairings

These protect the hands and upper body.

Windscreens

These protect the face and chest from the wind and rain.

Fig. 4.19   Handlebar fairings and windscreen

4. Clothing and Weather Protection

Handlebar muffs

These protect the hands only.

Fig. 4.20   Handlebar muffs

5. The Motorcycle Controls

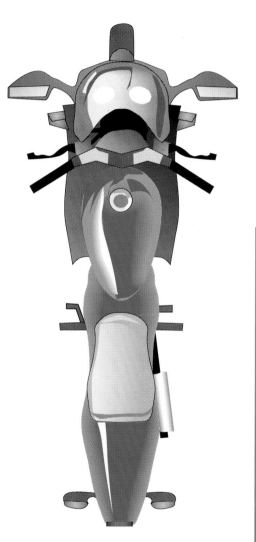

Motorcycles have various types of control. Most of these are for routine use, but some are for emergencies.

Most motorcycles have their controls in similar positions, but there are important differences.

For example, some mopeds have automatic transmission. Others are semi automatic.

Before you learn to ride you must know the position and function of all controls. Their use should be second nature.

This section is a guide to the controls on a typical motorcycle.

5. The Motorcycle Controls

Mirrors

Electric starter

Indicator switch

Horn

Clutch

HONDA

CD250U

Gear selector

Foot rest

Fig. 5.1   Motorcycle from left side showing normal positions of controls

Mirrors

Ignition switch

Engine cut-out switch

Choke

Front brake lever

Accelerator

Kick-start

Fuel tap (under fuel tank)

Rear brake pedal

Fig. 5.2   Motorcycle from right side showing normal positions of controls

5. The Motorcycle Controls

Fuel Tap

Controls the flow of fuel from the fuel tank to the engine.

The fuel tap has ON and OFF positions. If the fuel tank has reserve capacity, the fuel tap will also have a RESERVE position.

Many motorcycles have vacuum-operated fuel taps which do not need to be switched off (see your motorcycle handbook).

Position

Usually near or under the fuel tank.

Use

Always turn the fuel tap OFF when you are filling the tank or leaving your bike.

Fig. 5.3   Fuel tap

Fig. 5.4   Ignition switch

Ignition switch

The ignition switch controls the electrical supply so the engine can be started or stopped. The switch is usually operated by a key.

Position

Usually on the instrument panel.

Use

The ON and OFF positions are usually marked

- Switch to ON before you operate the starter
- When leaving your bike, switch to OFF and take the key with you

Choke

Helps when starting a cold engine.

The choke controls the amount of air in the fuel mixture. Operate the choke to

- Reduce the air in the mixture
- Increase the fuel to make the mixture 'rich'. A rich mixture makes cold starting easier.

Position

On the instrument panel, handlebar or on the carburettor(s).

Use

Operate the choke when you're starting the engine from cold.

Look this up in your motorcycle handbook.

Fig. 5.5   Choke

Caution

Make sure you return the choke to the 'off' position when the engine is warm. Leaving it on could cause excess wear to the engine. It also wastes fuel.

Starter

To turn the engine over and enable it to start.

Electric starter button

Position

On handlebar.

Use

1. Put gear lever in neutral (see Gear Selector)
2. Make sure the cut-out button is in the 'on' position
3. Switch on ignition
4. Press starter button

Kick-start lever

Position

Usually on right side of bike, just behind or in front of the footrest.

Use

1. Put gear lever in neutral (see Gear Selector)
2. Make sure the cut-out button is in the 'on' position
3. Switch on ignition
4. Fold out kick-start lever. You may need to hold up footrest.
5. Push down sharply with foot. Repeat until engine starts.

6. Fold kick-start lever back

Fig. 5.6   Electric starter

Fig. 5.7   Kick start

Fig. 5.8   Clutch

Clutch

Manual transmission only

The clutch lever engages and disengages the engine from the rear wheel (the driving wheel).

Smooth clutch control is the sign of a good rider.

This helps

- To change gears, or
- To select neutral and allow the bike to stand with the engine running
- To prevent the engine stalling when you're stopping

You should use the clutch lever when changing gear.

Position

On left handlebar

Use

To change gear

1. Squeeze clutch lever towards handlebar to disengage clutch
2. Select gear required

3. Release clutch lever smoothly to engage clutch

Fully automatic bikes

These have no clutch lever.

You simply select the mode you want: DRIVE or NEUTRAL

Semi-automatic bikes

These have no clutch lever.

The clutch operates automatically when you use the gear change pedal.

5. The Motorcycle Controls

Gear selector

Gears enable you to match engine power to road speed.

Low gears give higher engine power and lower road speed. Use these when you're moving off, climbing hills, or speeding up.

High gears give lower engine power and higher road speed. Use these when you're cruising.

Position

Usually on the left side of the bike just in front of the foot rest.

Some mopeds and scooters have a twist grip gearchange with the clutch lever on the left handlebar.

To select gear

On motorcycles the gears are selected by lifting or pushing down the gear lever with your foot. The positions and number of gears vary with the make of motorcycle.

Fig. 5.9 Gear selector

Neutral

The neutral position is when no gear is engaged. Some bikes have a warning light to show when the gears are in neutral.

Fig. 5.10 Throttle

Always work the throttle progressively, smoothly, gently.

Accelerator (throttle)

The throttle controls the engine speed by increasing or decreasing the amount of fuel used.

Position

A twist grip on the right handlebar

Use

To speed up engine: twist grip towards you.

To slow down engine: twist grip away from you.

When released, most throttles spring back to a position where the engine runs slowly ('idling speed').

Indicator switch

To operate direction indicators for left or right turns.

Position

Usually fitted on handlebar.

Use

Use to show you intend to change direction. Make sure to cancel the indicator after turning. Motorcycle indicators are seldom self-cancelling.

Fig. 5.11 Indicator switch

Light switch

Controls the lights.

A separate switch allows you to select main or dipped beam.

Position

Usually on handlebar.

Fig. 5.13   Light switch

Instrument panel

To give you information you need to ride

- Safely
- Within the law
- Taking care of your bike

Engine cut-out switch

To stop engine in emergency.

Position

Usually on right handlebar.

Use

To stop engine: hold cut-out in OFF position until engine stops.

Position

Usually a cluster of instruments between the handlebars.

Instruments usually include

- Speedometer giving the road speed in miles per hour and kilometres per hour
- Rev. counter giving the engine speed in revolutions per minute

Fig. 5.12   Engine cut-out switch

Then turn off the ignition. When you're leaving your bike, take the key.

- Warning lights, including
  - indicator repeater light
  - oil pressure light
  - 'gear in neutral' light
  - lights, etc.
- Ignition switch

Fig. 5.14   Instrument panel

5. The Motorcycle Controls

Brakes

Front brake lever

Applies brake to front wheel.

Position

On right handlebar just in front of grip.

Fig. 5.15   Front brake lever

Fig. 5.16   Rear brake pedal

Use

To apply the front brake: squeeze lever towards you. Always use all the fingers on your right hand for maximum control and stopping power.

To release brake: relax grip on lever.

Rear brake pedal

Applies brake to rear wheel.

Position

Usually on right side of bike, just in front of the footrest.

Some automatic machines have the rear brake lever on the left handlebar.

Use

To apply brake, press pedal with your foot.

To release brake, release pedal.

Mirrors

Enable you to see the road behind you.

Position

Usually on handlebars or fairing.

Flat mirrors

• Smaller view
• Easier to judge the speed and distance of traffic behind

Convex mirrors

• Larger view
• Harder to judge the speed and distance of traffic behind

Fig. 5.17   Convex & flat mirrors

Adjustment

Adjust to give the best view of the road behind.

You may need to extend the mirrors to make sure your body doesn't cause avoidable blind spots.

Horn

To warn other road users of your presence.

Position

Usually a button switch on the left handlebar.

Fig. 5.18   Horn

The regulations governing learner riders now call for compulsory training to be satisfactorily completed before you are allowed to ride on the road on your own.

This training can only be given by Approved Training Bodies and includes thorough off-road training to ensure that you are fully able to handle a motorcycle before venturing out for instruction on the public road.

A learner must complete each stage before starting the next.

Today's learners must be a lot more skilled much earlier in their riding careers than those in the past, and the standard of riding should be greatly improved among beginners.

This section outlines the main features of the compulsory training course. See also pages 8 – 11 of section 2.

6. Compulsory Basic Training

Learning to ride — compulsory basic training

Compulsory basic training was introduced on 1 December 1990 for

- All new learner motor-cyclists, including those who wish to ride motorcycles with sidecars
- All new learner moped riders

Approved Training Bodies

You must attend a course given by an Approved Training Body. These have

- Instructors who have passed the Driving Standards Agency course
- Sites approved by the Driving Standards Agency for off-road training

The Certificate of Completion

To gain a Certificate of Completion of Training, you must

- Reach a satisfactory standard in each of five elements (see pages 45-49)
- Complete these in sequence, finishing with an on-road section

Your instructor will not allow you to progress to the next element until you are ready to do so.

Local courses and training organisations

Ask about local courses at

- Your local council (Road Safety Officer)
- Your motorcycle dealer

Look in your local Yellow Pages under "Motorcycle training and testing"

Call 'Bikeline' (Freefone 0800-400 483) for a free information pack.

Element 1:
Introduction

Before you do any practical training you must understand

- The aims of the compulsory basic training course
- The importance of the right equipment and clothing
- The need to be clearly visible to other road users
- Legal requirements when riding on the road
- Why motorcyclists are more vulnerable than other road users
- The need to drive at correct speeds, according to road and traffic conditions
- The importance of reading and understanding the Highway Code

Eyesight

Your eyesight will be tested and you must be able to read a number-plate

- In good daylight
- Containing letters and figures 79.4 mm (3.1 inches) high
- At a distance of 20.5 metres (67 feet)
- With the aid of glasses or contact lenses if you normally wear them

Element 2:
Practical on-site
training

You must become familiar with the motorcycle, how it works, and how to use the controls. You must also be able to

- Carry out basic machine checks, and be able to take the bike on and off the stand

- Wheel your motorcycle around to the left and right showing proper balance, and stop the motorcycle by braking

- Stop and start the engine satisfactorily

Fig. 6.1

Element 3:
Practical on-site riding

You must be able to

- Ride your motorcycle under control in a straight line, and bring it to a controlled stop
- Ride your motorcycle in a figure of eight circuit
- Ride your motorcycle slowly under control
- Bring your motorcycle to a stop under full control as in an emergency
- Carry out controlled braking using both brakes
- Change gear satisfactorily
- Carry out rear observation correctly

- Carry out simulated left and right turns correctly using the routines

    - Observation-Signal-Manoeuvre (OSM)

The manoeuvre is broken down into Position-Speed-Look (PSL).

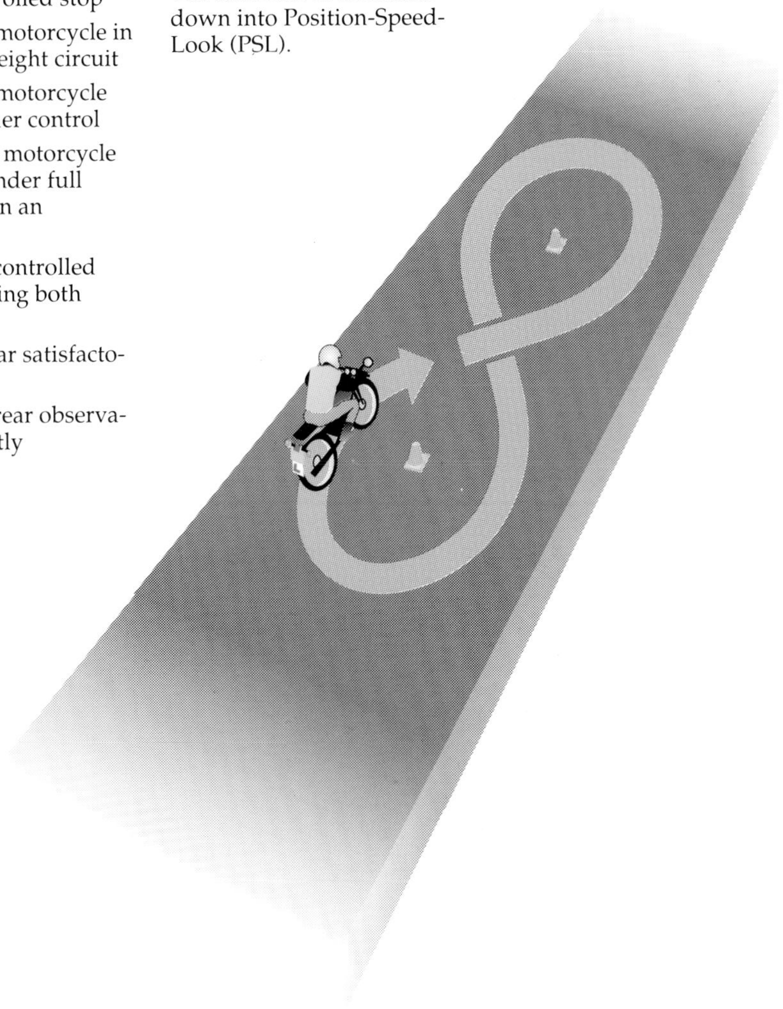

Fig. 6.2

6. Compulsory Basic Training

Element 4:
Practical on-road training

You must understand the need to, and be able to

- Ride defensively and anticipate the actions of other road users

- Use rear observation at appropriate times

- Assume the correct road position when riding

- Leave sufficient space when following another vehicle

- Pay due regard to the effect of varying weather when riding

- Be aware of the various types of road surfaces you can meet

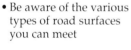

Fig. 6.3

Element 5: Practical on-road riding

You must be able to ride safely under a variety of road and traffic conditions including as many of the following as practicable

- Roundabouts
- Junctions
- Pedestrian crossings
- Traffic lights
- Gradients
- Bends
- Obstructions

DRIVING STANDARDS AGENCY

000000

Road Traffic Act 1988

Certificate of Completion of an Approved Training Course for Motor Vehicles in Categories A and P

Driver Number of Candidate

Hrs Mins

Date and time of course completion

Current name

Current address

Postcode

has successfully completed an approved training course for motor vehicles in categories A and P, prescribed for the purpose of Section 97 of the Road Traffic Act 1988 as amended by Section 6 of the Road Traffic (Driver Licensing and Information Systems) Act 1989.

Signature of Instructor — appointed to conduct such training

Initials and Surname (BLOCK CAPITALS) — No.

The successful candidate should sign in ink below in the presence of the instructor.

Signature

Official Stamp of Training Body

Site at which Course conducted and Site No.

Please read the notes overleaf

DL 196

An Executive Agency of the Department of Transport

CANCELLED

Fig. 6.4 Certificate of completion (DL196)

The Certificate of Completion

When you complete this element you will be given a Certificate of Completion of an Approved Training Course (Form DL196).

Keep this with you when you're riding. You'll have to show it to a police officer if asked to do so.

When you apply for a motorcycle or moped test, you must either

- Send this form with your application, or
- Present it to your driving examiner when you attend for your test

Note: Your test will be cancelled and you will lose the fee, if you fail to do so.

The Approved Training Body will also wish to talk to you about the need for further training to prepare you for your test.

As you read this section, you should bear in mind the requirements of Compulsory Basic Training (See Section 6).

If you are allowed to ride a moped without L-plates you are not bound to take Compulsory Basic Training but you are strongly advised to do so.

In this chapter, we take you step by step through the basics of motorcycle handling and control.

7. Starting to Ride

Stands

A stand will support the bike when you park it. Bikes have either a centre or side stand. Many bikes have both.

Centre stand

To take bike off centre stand

1. Stand on **left** of bike. Put your **right** foot in front of centre stand.
2. Hold left handlebar with your **left** hand. Hold the frame near the saddle with your **right** hand.
3. Pull bike forward, off stand.
4. Make sure stand is fully UP **before** you mount.

Warning

If the stand is not fully UP, it could dig into the road when you're cornering and cause an accident.

To put bike on centre stand

1. Stand on **left** of bike, holding the handlebar.
2. Push stand down with your **right** foot and hold the frame near the saddle. (Some machines have a special grab handle.)
3. Hold stand down with your right foot and pull bike backwards and upwards.

Fig. 7.1 Bike on centre stand

Side stand

To take bike off side stand

1. Stand on **left** of bike, holding the handlebar.
2. Push bike upright. Move the stand to its UP position, otherwise it could cause an accident.

Warning

If the stand is not fully UP, it could dig into the road when you're cornering and cause an accident.

To place bike on side stand

1. Stand on **left** of bike, holding the handlebar.
2. With bike upright, pull down stand with your **right** foot.
3. Pull bike towards you until its weight is resting on the stand.

Fig. 7.2   Bike on side stand

Mounting and dismounting

Make sure you apply the front brake while mounting and dismounting to prevent the bike from moving.

Practice

Practise mounting and dismounting with the bike off its stand.

Mounting and dismounting side

Always mount from the **left** of the bike, the side away from the traffic.

Adjusting the controls

Motorcycles are usually made for average-sized people, but you can adjust the main controls.

So you can use them comfortably and safely when you're riding, adjust

- Hand controls such as the frontbrake and clutch levers
- Foot controls such as the foot-brake lever and gear lever

Balancing and wheeling your bike

After you have practised mounting and dismounting, wheel the bike forward. Work the front brake with your right hand to control the speed.

Lean the bike towards you. This makes it easier to balance.

Practise wheeling the bike in circles both to the left and to the right, until you are able to balance and control it fully.

Fig. 7.3   Rider mounting

Riding position

Balance and control

When you are mounted on a stationary bike, you should be able to place both feet on the ground.

You should also be able to use one foot to keep your balance and the other to work the foot controls.

Fig. 7.4   Riding position (side view)

The best posture

Sit in a natural position, with your body leaning forward slightly.

You should be able to reach the hand controls comfortably.

Fig. 7.5   Riding position (front view)

7. Starting to Ride

Starting the Engine

To start engine

1. Push bike off its stand. Make sure the stand is fully UP. Mount the bike.
2. Make sure gear selector is at NEUTRAL. To check, push machine forward. If it is in neutral, the rear wheel will turn freely.

Some motorcycles have a light on the instrument panel to show that neutral is selected.

3. Turn fuel tap to ON.
4. If the engine is cold, move choke to ON (or CLOSED).
5. Make sure the engine cut-out switch is in ON position.
6. Turn ignition key to ON.
7. Open throttle slightly (not necessary on some bikes).

Your bike is now ready to start. The next step depends on whether your bike has an electric starter or a kick-start.

7. If your bike has an electric starter, press starter button. Go to step 9.
8. If your bike has a kick-start:

8.1 Fold out kick-start lever.

On some bikes you'll have to fold UP the footrest before you work the kick-start.

8.2 Place your instep on kick-start lever and push down sharply.

Allow kick-start lever to return to normal position carefully.

Repeat until engine starts.

8.3 Fold back kick-start lever immediately engine starts.

9. Open throttle control slightly to give a fairly high engine speed.
10. When engine is fully warm, move choke to OFF (or OPEN).

Stopping the engine

This safe sequence applies to most bikes.

1. Close throttle fully
2. Make sure gear selector is in NEUTRAL
3. Switch ignition to OFF. Take out key if you're leaving the bike.
4. Turn fuel tap to OFF, unless it's vacuum operated.

Riding means putting together all the aspects of your training: understanding the controls, handling your motorcycle, mounting, and so on.

If you're doing Compulsory Basic Training, you will not be allowed to ride on the road until you are ready to do so. You can still practise off-road.

This section deals with the basics of actually riding a moving motorcycle. Keep the CBT requirements in mind as you study it.

Section contents   page

8. Riding

Practising

For practice, choose a suitable place off the public road where you cause no danger or nuisance to anyone.

Training organisations have special areas for practice and some have motorcycles to hire for training.

Practise

- Starting and stopping when riding in a straight line, then
- Riding in circles to the left and right, making the circles gradually smaller
- Riding slowly, until you have mastered all the controls, turning, starting and stopping

Always keep both feet on the footrests. You must be able to turn safely to both the left and the right with **both** feet on the footrests.

You must also be able to work the clutch and throttle together and to brake safely. (See Fig. 8.1)

Balance

A motorcycle is harder to balance and keep upright than a bicycle. This is because motorcycles are much heavier. If your motorcycle falls on your leg it can injure you severely.

When riding

Never look down at the front wheel when riding. This can upset your balance.

Clutch control

Smooth clutch control is essential to good riding.

Biting point

You must be able to find the 'biting point' easily when releasing the clutch lever. The 'biting point' is the point where the engine begins to move the rear wheel.

Fig. 8.1

Safe moving off

To move off safely, follow these steps in this order

1. Sit astride your bike.
   - Apply front brake (right hand)
   - Start engine
2. Squeeze in clutch lever (Use all your fingers to get full control)
3. Select first gear (left foot). Keep clutch lever squeezed.
4. Put your left foot to the ground and shift the weight of the bike to that foot.

   Put your right foot on the footrest and apply rear brake.

You can now release the front brake and work the throttle.

5. Release clutch lever smoothly until you feel the engine trying to move the bike.

   Open the throttle slightly: just enough to keep the engine running smoothly.

You're now ready to move off.

6. Look over your right shoulder, unless you are moving off from the right hand side of the road, to make sure that
   - There is no traffic close to you
   - You are safe to move off
7. Signal if it will help other road users.
8. Gradually release clutch lever. At the same time open the throttle smoothly.

   As you move off, release the rear brake and bring your foot up on the footrest.

Fig. 8.2   Moving off safely

Using the gears

1. Push down on or lift the gear lever with the toe of your boot as far as it will go.
2. Allow the selector to return to its normal position after each change.

When to change

Experience will tell you when to change gear. Listening to the sound of the engine helps.

Never let the engine

- Race when you could change to a higher gear
- Labour when you could change to a lower gear

Gear changing

To change up or down you need to be able to co-ordinate clutch, throttle and gear lever

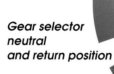

Gear selector neutral and return position

Fig. 8.3 Typical gear positions

Changing up

When you have reached the road speed you need to change up to the next gear.

1. At the same time
   - Close throttle
   - Pull in clutch lever
2. Select the next higher gear.
3. Release clutch lever smoothly.
4. Open throttle.
5. Repeat this sequence every time you change up.

Always travel in the highest gear you can for the road and traffic conditions. You'll save fuel and spare your engine.

Changing down

Experience will tell you the right moment to change down.

1. At the same time,
   - Close throttle until just slightly open
   - Pull in clutch lever
2. Select the next lower gear
3. At the same time,
   - Release clutch lever smoothly
   - Open throttle

Braking

Always look and plan well ahead to avoid having to brake firmly. A gradual increase of pressure on the brakes is better than late, harsh braking.

Follow these rules

1. Brake only when your machine is upright and moving in a straight line
2. Brake in good time
3. Adjust the pressure on the brakes according to the road surface and weather conditions.

Braking sequence

The front brake is the more powerful of the two brakes, and the most important in stopping a motorcycle.

To stop most effectively

1. Apply the front brake a fraction of a second before you apply the rear brake.
2. Apply a greater pressure to the front brake. That pressure will vary according to the road and weather conditions. Front brake pressure should be lighter in wet or slippery conditions.

This method gives greater stopping power because

- The weight of the bike and rider is thrown forward
- The front tyre is pressed more firmly on the road, giving a better grip

Make this method a habit.

Using both brakes

Many motorcycle riders are, quite wrongly, afraid to use the front brake. This is often as a result of what they were taught as cyclists.

On a motorcycle, **you must normally use both brakes**.

Using one brake only

Using the front or the rear brake only will

- Take you much longer to stop (See Fig. 8.5)
- Increase your chances of skidding

At very low speeds (walking pace) in heavy traffic, using the rear brake only gives smoother control. The more powerful front brake could upset your balance.

Braking on a bend

A good rider will plan well ahead to avoid braking on a bend.

If you must brake on a bend, use the rear brake only, but with extreme care to prevent the wheel locking.

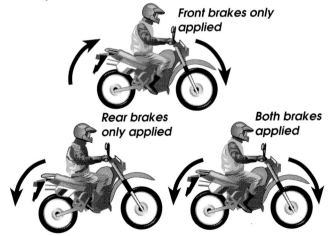

Front brakes only applied

Rear brakes only applied

Both brakes applied

Fig. 8.4 The effects of braking

Emergency braking

A good rider seldom needs to brake violently or stop suddenly, but you must be able to stop quickly and safely in an emergency.

To get maximum braking

1. Use the front brake slightly before the rear
2. Brake progressively (increase pressure steadily)
3. Apply the right amount of braking effort to each wheel. This will depend on the road surface and weather conditions (see previous page).

When braking in an emergency

You must

1. Keep your bike upright.
2. Apply maximum effort without locking the wheels. As you slow down, you might have to ease off on the brakes to avoid skidding.
3. Pull in clutch lever just before you stop.

Signalling when you brake

Don't try to give an arm signal when you brake in an emergency.

- You need both hands on the handlebars
- Your stop light will warn traffic behind you

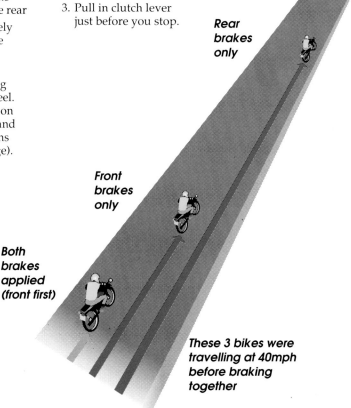

Rear brakes only

Front brakes only

Both brakes applied (front first)

These 3 bikes were travelling at 40mph before braking together

Fig. 8.5 Stopping distances using different brake combinations

Stopping safely

To stop safely, follow these steps in this order

1. Look over your right shoulder to check following traffic and make sure it is safe to slow down. Signal if it will help other road users.

2. Close throttle.

3. Apply brakes smoothly until bike stops.

4. Just before bike stops, pull in clutch lever to disengage clutch and avoid stalling engine.

5. As bike stops, put your left foot on the ground.

6. When bike has stopped,
   - Keep front brake applied
   - Release rear brake
   - Support bike with right foot

7. With clutch lever still pulled, select neutral (move gear lever with left foot)
   - Release clutch lever
   - Place both feet on the ground
   - Release front brake

Disengaging clutch

When stopping from very low road speeds, pull in clutch lever just before or just as you brake.

When stopping from higher road speeds, always brake first and pull in the clutch lever just before you stop.

The United Kingdom has a great variety of roads, from quiet country lanes to multiple lane motorways. Riding a motorcycle on some of these presents difficulties.

First of all, you must learn to handle your motorcycle on fairly standard, everyday roads, the kind you are most likely to find yourself riding on.

This section deals with the main features, hazards and demands of typical British roads.

9. Getting to Know the Road

The road surface

Recognising surface types

The state of the road surface is very important to motorcyclists.

Only a very small part of the motorcycle tyre is in contact with the road at any one time — about the area of the sole of a man's shoe. Any small change in the surface can affect the stability of the motorcycle.

Learn to recognise poor road surfaces.

Look out for

- Manhole covers
- Pot-holes
- Loose surfaces, such as leaves and gravel
- Oil patches, especially at roundabouts, bus stops and filling stations
- 'Banding' (Shiny lines of tarmac around road repairs)

Avoid poor surfaces where you can. If you can't avoid them, slow down.

Fig. 9.1 Riding over a poor surface

Road position

Best position

As a general rule, keep to the centre of the lane. On a single carriageway road, that is halfway between the centre of the road and the left side.

Your position should allow you to

- Be easily seen in the mirror of any vehicle immediately in front of you.
- Move over smoothly to the left if someone tries to squeeze past.

Keep clear of the gutter where there are often more pot-holes and loose grit.

Keep clear of the centre of the road. You might

- Obstruct traffic overtaking
- Put yourself in danger from oncoming traffic
- Encourage others to overtake you on your left

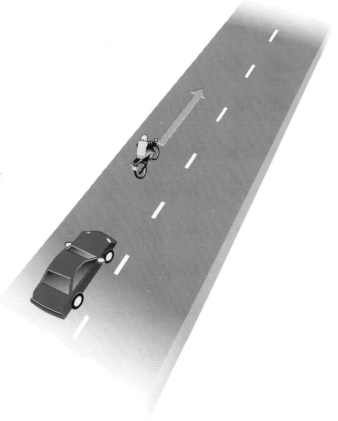

Fig. 9.2   Correct road position for normal riding

9. Getting to Know the Road

On bends

Roads are seldom straight for very long. They curve to suit the terrain. Bends can be deceptive.

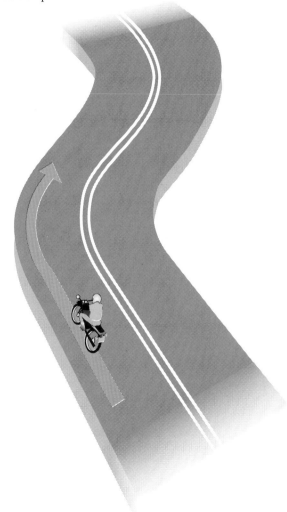

Fig. 9.3   Approaching right-hand bend

Watch out for

- Road signs warning you of a bend. (Highway Code, p54)
- The word SLOW on the road

If you have to slow down, do so in good time.

Select the correct gear and let the engine take you round at a constant speed.

Your view of the bend

High hedges, fences and walls can reduce your view. So read the road and adjust your speed to suit.

Be ready to stop!

Right-hand bend

Keep to left to improve your view. Watch out for

- Uneven surfaces
- Adverse camber

Choose your speed to suit.

Warning

On sharp right-hand bends, keep well to the left.

If you ride too close to the centre line, you might be too close to oncoming traffic and your head could be over the centre line and on the wrong side of the road.

Left-hand bend

Keep to your normal road position. Don't move out into the centre of the road where you may be too close to oncoming traffic.

The camber may be just right, but don't let that lure you into taking the bend too fast.

Fig. 9.4 Approaching left-hand bend

Braking

Where to brake

Where you brake is very important. The best time to brake is when you are travelling

- Upright
- In a straight line
- At a constant speed

Braking on bends

On a bend, the weight of bike and rider is thrown outwards. To balance this, the rider leans inwards slightly.

If you brake on a bend

- The weight will be thrown outwards even more
- Bike and rider may be thrown off balance

If you must brake on a bend

- Use the rear brake ONLY.
- Brake gently to avoid locking the wheel. A locked wheel loses grip on the road and skids sideways. You could easily come off.

Braking on bends increases the risk of skidding

Fig. 9.5   The effects of braking on bends

Skidding

A skid is when one or both tyres

- Lose their grip on the road surface
- Veer off the steered course, and/or
- Prevent the brakes working (by sliding over the road surface)

What causes skidding?

- Heavy or uncoordinated braking, which locks one or both wheels
- A sudden increase in engine speed, causing wheel spin
- A sudden change of direction
- Leaning over at too great an angle when cornering, causing one or both tyres to loose grip

A good rider tries to avoid getting into a skid.

That's a lot easier than getting out of one.

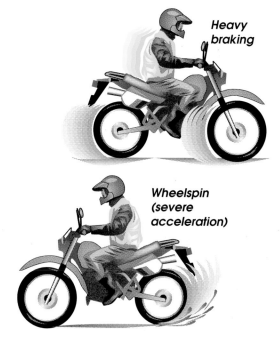

Heavy braking

Wheelspin (severe acceleration)

Swerving (changing direction suddenly)

Leaning too far over when cornering

Fig. 9.6   The causes of skidding

9. Getting to Know the Road

Avoiding skids

- Try to avoid riding on slippery surfaces. If you have to do so, slow down well in advance.
- If you find yourself on a slippery surface, do not brake or swerve suddenly. Check the traffic, then gradually slow down.
- Avoid manhole covers and drains, especially in the wet.

Take care on

- Level crossings and over wood-block surfaces or cobbles especially when wet.
- Parking areas and lay-bys where heavy vehicles often stand and leave oil patches.
- Approaches to junctions, where frequent braking and acceleration can polish the surface, making it hazardous.

Take particular care when riding on loose chippings.

Watch other traffic. If they're driving slowly and cautiously, that could mean the road is slippery.

a. Manhole cover

b. Tar 'banding'

Fig. 9.7 Skid hazards

c. Oil patch

The Motorcycling Manual

Dealing with skids

They can happen suddenly. You must know how to control them.

Sudden acceleration

- If you've caused rear-wheel skid by sudden acceleration, ease off the throttle.
- Wheel spin can cause the bike to slide sideways just the same as a locked wheel can.

Braking

The natural reaction to a skid is to brake.

- Don't brake. Let the wheels keep turning.
- If you've caused the skid by braking and locking one or both wheels, ease off the brake.

Bike skidding to the left

Direction of steering to correct skid

- **Ease off brake**
- **Steer to left**

Fig. 9.8   Action to correct a skid

Correcting a skid

- Steer into the skid. If the bike is sliding to the right, steer to the right, if the bike is sliding to the left, steer to the left.
- Keep your feet on the footrests. Putting a foot to the ground could upset your balance, and won't steady the bike unless you are going very slowly.

9. Getting to Know the Road

Stopping distance

You must know the stopping distance at all speeds. Ride at a speed which allows you to stop safely in the distance you can see clearly ahead.

Definition

Stopping distance is the total distance from the point you first see the hazard to the point where you come to a complete stop.

For example, on a good dry road, the stopping distance at 50 mph is about 175 feet (53 metres).

Stopping distance divides into two: thinking distance and braking distance.

Thinking distance

The distance from the point where you see the hazard to the point where you begin to brake.

Thinking distance varies from rider to rider, according to physical and mental condition, time of day and so on.

An alert and fit rider needs .75 of a second thinking time. That means at 50 mph you'll travel 50 feet **before you begin to brake**.

So, the thinking distance at 50 mph is 50 feet (15 metres).

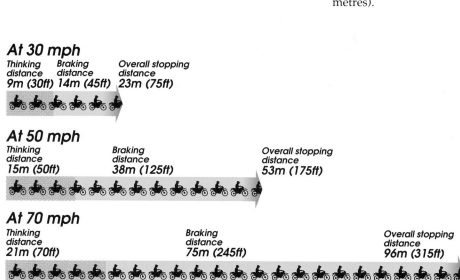

At 30 mph
Thinking distance
9m (30ft)
Braking distance
14m (45ft)
Overall stopping distance
23m (75ft)

At 50 mph
Thinking distance
15m (50ft)
Braking distance
38m (125ft)
Overall stopping distance
53m (175ft)

At 70 mph
Thinking distance
21m (70ft)
Braking distance
75m (245ft)
Overall stopping distance
96m (315ft)

Fig. 9.9   Stopping distance chart

The Motorcycling Manual

Braking distance

The distance you travel from the point where you begin to brake and the point where you come to a complete stop.

Braking distance varies with road conditions, brake efficiency and so on.

At 50 mph, the braking distance is 125 feet (38 metres) on a good dry road.

As speed increases

Stopping distance goes up dramatically as you increase your road speed.

At 30 mph

The stopping distance is 75 feet (23 metres).

At 70 mph

The stopping distance is 315 feet (96 metres).

That's **just over double** the speed but **more than four times** the stopping distance. (See Fig. 9.10)

A wet or icy road could mean much longer stopping distances.

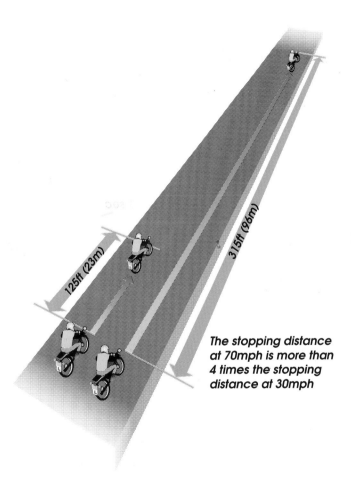

The stopping distance at 70mph is more than 4 times the stopping distance at 30mph

Fig 9.10   Increase in stopping distance as speed increases

Separation distance

How far must you keep from the vehicle in front? Ideally you should be no closer than the stopping distance that corresponds to your speed.

In congested traffic that may not be reasonable. Even then, the gap must never be less than your thinking distance, and much more if the road is wet or slippery.

A useful guide on an open road in good conditions is to allow a gap of one yard (1 metre) for each mph of your speed: for example 45 yards (45 metres) at 45mph.

A useful technique for judging one metre per mph is to use the 'two second rule'.

The two-second rule

A skilful rider in good conditions needs to be at least two seconds behind the vehicle in front.

How to measure

1. Select an obvious stationary object, a telegraph pole or road sign, for example.

2. As the vehicle in front passes it, say to yourself, 'only a fool breaks the two-second rule!'

If you reach the object **before** you finish saying it, you're **too close**.

In bad weather, keep at least double the safety gap between you and the vehicle in front.

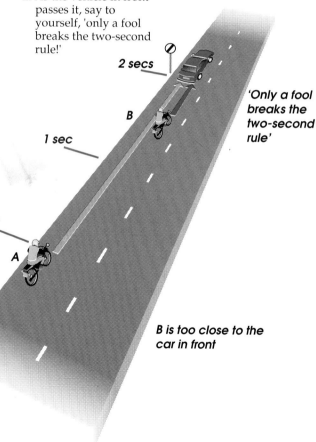

2 secs

B

1 sec

start

A

'Only a fool breaks the two-second rule'

B is too close to the car in front

Fig. 9.11   Separation distances

Separation distance behind you

When the vehicle behind is following too closely, slow down gradually and increase the gap between you and the vehicle in front. This allows

- You plenty of time to brake, if necessary
- The vehicle following to overtake

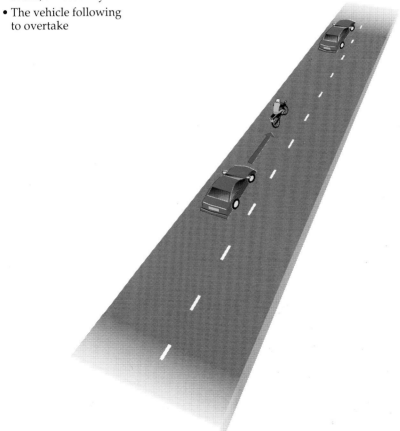

Fig. 9.12 Separation distance behind

Parking

The parking rules in the Highway Code also apply to motorcycles. However, you need to take special care when parking your motorcycle.

- Park on firm and level ground. Soft ground might cause the stand to sink and the bike to fall over.

  On a very hot day, side or centre stands can sink into tarmac softened by the heat.

On uneven ground your bike might also fall over. In either case a passer-by might be injured or your bike damaged.

- Use the centre stand if you are leaving your bike for some time

- Switch off the fuel tap and lock the steering (or use a chain and padlock)

- Take the ignition key with you

- Avoid leaving a side-car outfit on a gradient.
  If you must do so, block a wheel or wedge it against the kerb to prevent the motorcycle running away.

- Leave the machine in low gear

Fig. 9.13a. Correctly parked

Fig. 9.13b. Incorrectly parked

Fig. 9.13c. Correctly parked

Fig. 9.13d. Incorrectly parked

Defensive Riding is based on good observation and anticipation. It's about always questioning the actions of other road users.

On today's roads, it's important that you look and plan well ahead, and are not taken by surprise. If you expect the unexpected and try to anticipate the actions of other road users, you're less likely to be caught out.

If there's danger ahead, it's also important that you don't try to do too many things at once. You must take them in sequence.

This section describes the main features of Defensive Riding. Use the technique whenever you ride.

10. Defensive Riding

Observation

Zone of vision

The area you can see from your riding position. When you are on the move, this keeps changing.

A skilful rider constantly watches what's happening ahead.

If you can't see far enough ahead, **slow down and be prepared to stop.**

At a junction

The zone of vision at a junction includes your view into other roads.

This usually improves as you get nearer, but is often limited. You may need to get close before you can look far enough into other roads to see if it's safe to go across.

At some junctions, your view may be so restricted that you need to stop and inch forward for a proper view before you emerge.

- Look in every direction before you emerge.
- Keep looking as you join the other road.

Approaching a bend

Ask yourself

- How sharp is it?
- Is my speed right?
- Am I in the right position?
- What might I meet?

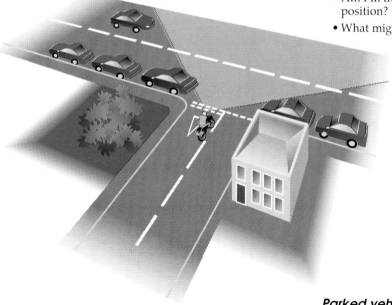

Parked vehicles near a junction

Fig. 10.1 shows how parked vehicles can limit vision at junctions.

Fig 10.1   Parked vehicles can limit vision at a junction

Approaching a junction

Ask yourself

- Can other drivers see me?
- Am I sure they have seen me?
- Have I an escape route if they haven't?

Remember

Poor drivers may not look long enough to ensure they have seen you. They may not 'Think Bike'. Daytime use of your dipped headlamps will increase the chances of you being seen.

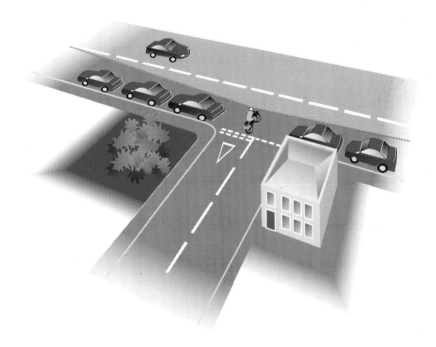

Fig. 10.2 Inch forward to get a better view

10. Defensive Riding

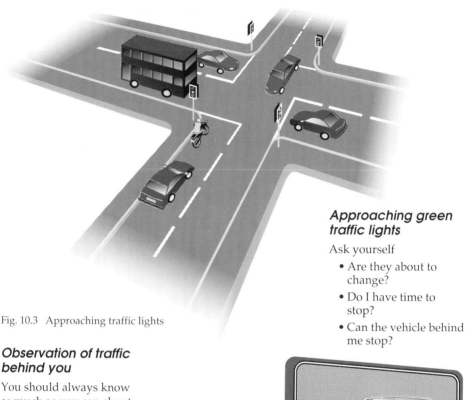

Fig. 10.3 Approaching traffic lights

Observation of traffic behind you

You should always know as much as you can about the traffic behind you.

Before you change direction or speed, you must know how your action will affect drivers following.

You must also be aware of traffic likely to overtake or come alongside you.

You have two methods of checking traffic behind you: looking behind and using mirrors. See p83.

Approaching green traffic lights

Ask yourself

- Are they about to change?
- Do I have time to stop?
- Can the vehicle behind me stop?

Fig. 10.4 Mirror view of traffic behind

Looking behind

Why look behind?

Even if your motorcycle has mirrors, they don't always give a full rear view.

There are times when you need to look round to fully determine the speed, position and course of following traffic.

Looking behind also warns other drivers that you may be about to signal or alter course.

When should you look behind?

Well before you signal your intention or make any manoeuvre. For example, before

- Moving off
- Changing direction
- Turning right or left
- Overtaking
- Changing lanes
- Slowing or stopping

Normally, look over your right shoulder, but you'll need to look over your left shoulder before moving or turning to the left.

Looking over your shoulder too often can be hazardous.

The 'Lifesaver' glance

A final quick rearward glance into the blind area before altering course. As the name suggests it could save your life.

Never forget to use it!

Warning

Looking behind can be hazardous when you're riding at high speed on the open road or in congested moving traffic.

In the time you take to look behind, you not only lose touch with what's going on in front but also run the risk of veering off course.

In these circumstances, combine

- **Regular and sensible use of the mirrors, with**

- **The "Lifesaver" glance into the blind area before altering course**

Fig. 10.5 The 'Lifesaver' glance

Mirrors

Mirrors must be

- Of a suitable type, and not likely to be a danger to the rider
- Free of vibration
- Clean and free of dust or grime
- Properly adjusted to give a clear view behind

Note: You may need to extend the mirrors so that your body doesn't create blind spots.

Types of mirror

Mirrors can be flat or convex. See Section 6 for more details.

Using the Mirrors

Glancing in your mirrors regularly enables you to keep up-to-date with what is happening behind you without losing touch with what's going on in front.

Just looking is not enough!

Whether you look in the mirrors or over your shoulder, just looking is not enough. You must act sensibly on what you see, and take note of the speed, behaviour and possible intentions of traffic behind.

10. Defensive Riding

Signals

Signal to
- Help other road users
- Warn them of your intention

Road users include
- Drivers of following and oncoming vehicles
- Cyclists
- Pedestrians
- Crossing supervisors
- Police directing traffic

Give **only** correct signals. (See Figs. 10.6 & 10.8)

Signal clearly and in good time!

Types of Signals

Arm signals

Very effective in daylight when you are wearing bright fluorescent clothing.

Giving any arm signal means that you have less steering control, if only briefly. You must practise controlling your bike while giving arm signals.

Practise
- With one hand and then with the other
- Before you venture out on the road

Timing an arm signal

Don't try to keep up an arm signal all through a turn, as you would with direction indicators. You need **both** hands on the handlebars as you turn.

Arm signals at speed

When travelling at speed on the open road, you won't find it safe to extend your arm fully, so use your direction indicators.

I intend to move out to the right or turn right

I intend to move in to the left or turn left

I intend to slow down or to stop

Signals to traffic controllers

I want to turn right

I want to turn left

I want to go straight on

Fig. 10.6   Arm signals

Arm signal at pedestrian crossings.

Always use an arm signal when slowing down or stopping at pedestrian crossings. This not only tells following and approaching traffic that you're stopping, but also waiting pedestrians. They can't see your brake light.

However you signal, you must do all you can to ensure that following traffic knows what you intend to do before you do it.

Fig. 10.7 Signalling at crossing

Direction indicator signals

Indicator lamps are close together on a motorcycle, so help other road users to understand your intention by

• Positioning yourself correctly and in good time for the manoeuvre you intend to take

• On some smaller machines, the direction indicators do not show up very well in bright sunlight. Give an arm signal as well, just to be sure.

I intend to move in to the left or turn left or stop on the left

I intend to move out to the right or turn right

I am slowing down or stopping

Fig. 10.8 Indicator signals

10. Defensive Riding

Conflicting signals

Holding the left arm straight out means 'I am going to move in to the left or turn left', **not** 'I am going to stop on the left'. Use the correct arm signal if you intend to stop. (See Fig. 10.6)

A signal with the left indicator means 'I am going to turn left' OR 'I am going to stop on the left'.

Avoid using your left indicator if you intend to stop on the left just after a left-hand junction. A driver waiting at that junction might think you are turning left and drive into your path.

Either

• Wait until you've **passed** the junction, then indicate that you intend to stop, or

• Reduce speed by braking gently, so that your brake light warns following drivers

I intend to move in to the left or turn left or stop on the left

Fig. 10.9   Conflicting signals

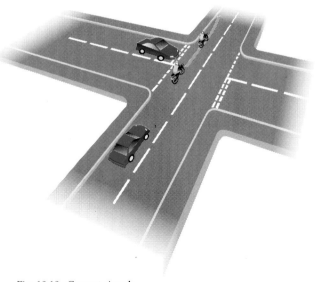

Fig. 10.10   Correct signals

Other signals

Stop lamps

Most drivers react very quickly when they see the stop lamps light up on the vehicle ahead. So

- Brake in good time
- Slow down gradually
- Help other road users by giving an earlier signal
- If necessary, let them know your intention even earlier by giving an arm signal

Horn

There are few situations when you'll need to use the horn. Using the horn does not

- Give you the right of way
- Relieve you of your responsibility to ride safely. Sound it only if
  - you think someone may not have seen you
  - you want to warn of your presence, for example at blind bends or junctions

Never use your horn as a rebuke, or to attract a friend's attention!

Don't use your horn when stationary, except in an emergency.

On high speed roads

Drivers on high-speed roads may not hear you coming up behind them. Don't rely on them hearing your horn either.

In daylight, they are more likely to be aware of you if you are using dipped headlamps.

Flashing with headlamps

Use only as an alternative to the horn to remind others that you're there. Assume that other drivers mean the same.

Don't flash at anyone to go ahead or turn!

If someone flashes their headlamps at you

Before you act on the signal, make sure

- You understand what they mean
- It is you they are signalling

Never assume it's a signal to proceed.

When signalling, always

- Signal in good time
- Signal clearly
- Signal correctly

Safe moving off and changing course is your responsibility.

10. Defensive Riding

Hazards

A hazard is any situation which involves you in some risk or danger.

To identify a hazard you must look well ahead for

- Road signs
- Changes in road conditions
- Parked vehicles
- Junctions
- Cyclists
- Pedestrians
- Horse riders
- Animals, particularly dogs off the lead

Action when approaching a hazard

The action you need to take will vary from one hazard to another. Any action which demands a change of speed or course is called a manoeuvre.

A manoeuvre can vary from slowing slightly to turning on a very busy road.

Manoeuvring

Observation-Signal-Manoeuvre (OSM)

Follow this drill every time you approach a hazard. See Figure 10.11.

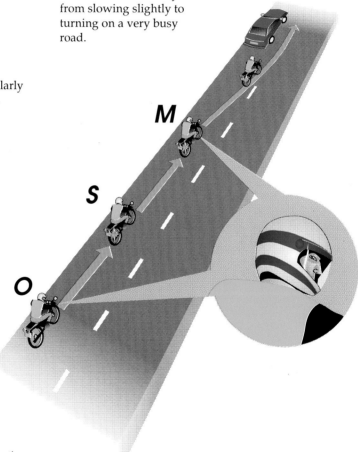

Fig. 10.11   The OSM routine

Observation

Check the position of traffic following you.

Signal

If necessary, signal your intention to change course or slow down.

Signal clearly and in good time.

Manoeuvre

Carry out the manoeuvre if it is safe to do so.

Manoeuvring has three phases, Position-Speed-Look (PSL)

$$M \begin{cases} \textbf{Look} \\ \textbf{Speed} \\ \textbf{Position} \end{cases}$$

Signal
(right-hand indicator)

Rear observation

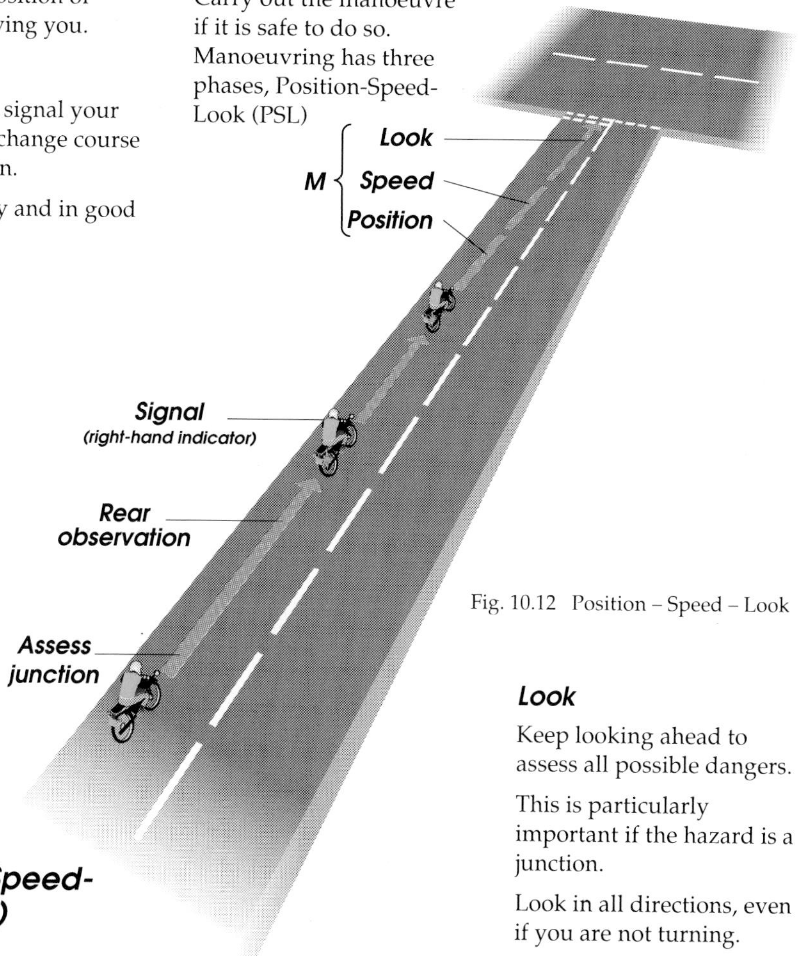

Fig. 10.12 Position – Speed – Look

Assess junction

Look

Keep looking ahead to assess all possible dangers.

This is particularly important if the hazard is a junction.

Position-Speed-Look (PSL)

Position

Get into the correct position in good time to negotiate the hazard. This helps other road users to see what you intend to do.

Positioning yourself too late can be dangerous.

Speed

Slow down as you approach a hazard.

Always be ready to stop.

Look in all directions, even if you are not turning.

If you are joining a road, keep looking as you turn from one road to the other.

Watch out for
- Traffic turning across your path
- Pedestrians

10. Defensive Riding

Spotting hazards

Events can happen

- At the same time, OR
- In quick succession

In Figure 10.13 the rider must pull out to pass the stationary lorry, but

- Is the blue car really going to turn left? The driver may have forgotten to cancel the indicator from a previous turn.
- If the blue car does turn, will the pedestrian decide to cross?
- When will the rider see the red car, which may want to turn left?

When travelling fast, you are not likely to be able to cope with all those events at once.

So, other road users, who may not be doing anything wrong, can turn an easy piece of riding into a hazard.

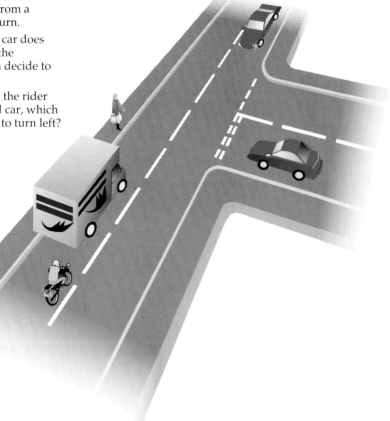

Fig. 10.13 Anticipating hazards

Allowing time and space

Always leave yourself enough time and space to cope with what's ahead.

- Keep your eyes moving
- Look far ahead and near, especially in town where things change quickly
- Check regularly on what's following you
- Watch for clues about what's going to happen next

For example

A parked car could spell danger, if

- The driver or a passenger is sitting in it, OR
- The engine is running: watch for exhaust smoke

Remember that

- A door might open suddenly, OR
- The car might pull out without warning

Watch out for pedestrians who may rush out between parked vehicles.

Heavy and slow-moving traffic

Don't weave between lines of slow moving traffic unless you have enough room to allow

- Doors to open
- Pedestrians to cross

DON'T

Get too close behind a van or large goods vehicle. The driver might not be able to see you, or the vehicle might roll back.

Your safety

Your safety lies largely in your own hands. The better your control of bike and roadspace, the safer you'll be.

It's especially important to stay in control in tricky road and traffic conditions on a bike with more power than you're used to.

Positioning

Ask yourself
- Can I see and be seen?
- Are other vehicles restricting my course of action?
- Have I enough room to get out of trouble?

Speed

Ask yourself
- Could I stop in time if the vehicle in front braked sharply?
- Am I going too fast for the road?
- Am I in the right gear to get myself out of a tight spot?

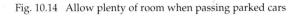

Fig. 10.14   Allow plenty of room when passing parked cars

10. Defensive Riding

Lighting conditions

Even in the dark, you can see that you're approaching a hazard.

Look for

- Illuminated signs
- Reflective signs
- Reflectors between white lines
- The glow of vehicle headlamps on trees and buildings indicating a corner or junction

Be careful

- It can be difficult to judge distances and speed from headlamps.
- At night, bright lights on some vehicles make it difficult to see less bright lights, such as cyclists or low-powered motorcycles.
- Don't let shop and advertising lights distract you. Keep a good look out for zebra crossings, traffic lights and other road users.

Wet roads

- Increase reflected and distracting light
- Make unlit objects even less visible

Rain

Makes headlamps less effective at night. On dark and poorly lit roads, slow down and watch for unlit objects . For example, builder's skips or parked cars. Generally, ride more slowly in rain.

Unlit side view

You will be sideways on to other drivers when you're

- Passing side turnings
- Turning right

This means you will be seen less easily. Wearing reflective material will help.

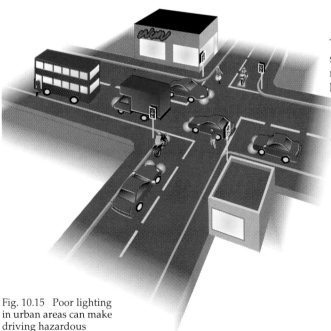

Fig. 10.15   Poor lighting in urban areas can make driving hazardous

Cyclists

Make allowances for cyclists.

The younger the cyclist the more you must watch them.

Cyclists might

- Glance round, showing they might be about to move out or turn
- Make sudden sideways movements into your path
- Be carrying light but bulky objects which may affect their control and balance
- Weave about, slow down, or stop and get off on a hill

Pedestrians

When turning from one road to another

- Always look out for pedestrians
- Give way to any who are crossing

At pedestrian crossings

Never overtake within the zig zag area of a zebra or pelican pedestrian crossing.

Children

Take extra care where children may be about, particularly in residential areas, near schools and parks.

Look out for parked ice cream vans — children are more interested in ice cream than they are in traffic.

Disabled pedestrians

Take special care with the visually handicapped, the old, or disabled.

Remember a deaf person is not easy to identify.

Take extra care if a pedestrian fails to look your way as you approach.

Animals

Animals are easily frightened by

- Noise
- Vehicles coming close to them

Ride

- Slowly and quietly — don't sound the horn
- Keeping engine speed low — don't 'rev'

Give animals as much room as possible.

Horses

Be particularly careful when approaching horses especially when ridden by children.

Persons in charge of animals

If someone in charge of animals signals to you to stop, do so and switch off your engine.

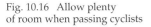

Fig. 10.16 Allow plenty of room when passing cyclists

10. Defensive Riding

Road surfaces

Anticipating conditions

Motorcyclists need to be much more concerned with the road condition than car drivers.

Stay alert to the road surface ahead, you might have to brake.

Ask yourself

- Is the road wet, greasy, worn or uneven?
- Are there any metal covers or surfaces ahead?
- Can I keep my bike upright and avoid skidding?

Wet roads

If the surface is good but wet

- Aim to brake when the machine is in its most stable position. That is upright and moving straight ahead.
- Apply the front brake slightly before the rear. Spread the braking effort evenly between the front and rear.

Remember! A wet road means

- Less efficient braking
- A longer distance needed to stop
- A greater risk of skidding

Ride more slowly on a wet road and take extra care.

Wherever you ride today, you are going to have to deal with traffic. This could be on heavily congested urban roads or in light traffic on rural roads.

You must know how to cope safely with the problems modern day traffic presents.

This section outlines the problems of riding in traffic and the techniques you must learn to ride safely.

11. Riding in Traffic

Road Junctions

A junction is where two or more roads meet

Types of junction

There are five main types

1. T junctions
2. Y junctions
3. Staggered junctions
4. Crossroads
5. Roundabouts

Junction indicators

Look for indications of a junction ahead, such as

- Warning signs
- Road markings
- Direction signs
- Priority signs
- GIVE WAY and STOP signs
- Traffic lights
- A break in the line of buildings
- A change in road surface

Junctions

T ,Y, staggered & crossroads

How you approach a junction depends on what you intend to do. You might want to

- Cross a main road going ahead
- Emerge into a main road by turning right
- Emerge into a main road by turning left
- Leave a main road by turning right or left into a side road
- Stay on a main road and pass the junction

A main road is one with priority over another at a junction. Road signs and markings usually indicate a main road.

Caution
The road surface at junctions

Always check

- For slippery surfaces or loose chippings
- That it is safe to accelerate away from the junction.

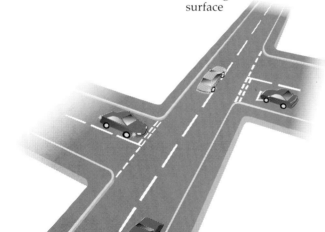

Fig 11.1 Approaching a staggered junction

Be seen!
Use dipped headlamps at all times.

Approaching a junction

At every junction use OSM/PSL routine. See page 88.

- Observation — look round to see what's behind.
- Signal — clearly in good time
- Manoeuvre - use PSL
- Position — correctly and in good time

If the road has no lane markings

When turning left — keep well to the left, about 3 feet from the kerb.

When turning right — keep as close to the centre of the road as is safe.

In a one-way street — move to the right-hand side of the road as early as you can.

If the road has lane markings

Use the correct lane for the direction you intend to take and move into it as soon as you can.

- Speed — adjust speed as necesssary
- Look — look out for other traffic when you reach a point from which you can see.

Position of vehicles

Don't

- Be tempted to ride between lines of vehicles
- Switch lanes to gain advantage over others.

When you move ahead

- Do so in the correct lane for the direction you intend to take
- Look out for signals from vehicles about to change lanes

- Look out for vehicles suddenly changing lanes without signalling.

Articulated or long vehicles

These need much more room than cars, and may take up a position that seems wrong to you.

Stay clear of large vehicles at junctions.

Don't be tempted to squeeze by. The rear wheels might cut across your path.

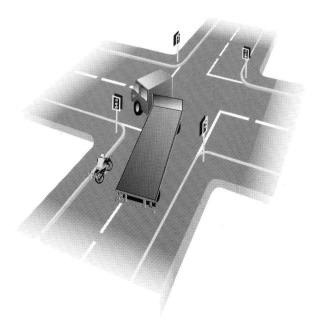

Fig. 11.2   Watch out at junctions for large vehicles turning

Emerging

When a rider leaves one road and joins or crosses another, this is called 'emerging'.

You will have to decide when it is necessary to wait and when it is safe to go. That decision depends largely on your zone of vision (See page 80).

You can only decide to 'wait or go on' when you have put yourself in a position where you can see clearly.

Being able to judge the speed and distance of other traffic is essential: you must not force another driver to change plans.

Remember!

You must be careful to join or cross the path of other traffic only when they are far enough away to make it safe to do so. This not only requires great care but often a lot of patience too!

When turning right

Don't be tempted to ride alongside other vehicles hoping to fit in to a gap in the traffic.

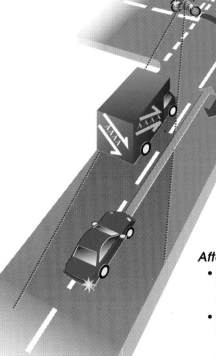

After you emerge

- Check behind for the speed and position of other traffic.
- Check that your speed is correct for the road and conditions.
- Keep a safe distance from the vehicle in front.
- Don't attempt to overtake until you have had time to assess the conditions on the new road.

Fig. 11.3 Dangers when emerging to turn right

Turning left into a major road

- Assess the junction. Check the road signs and markings.
- Use OSM/PSL routine.

O – Look in your mirrors and over your right shoulder to assess what's behind.

S – Signal left at the correct time.

M – Manoeuvre, use PSL

P – Keep well to the left, about 3ft from the kerb

S – Reduce speed. Be prepared to stop: traffic on a minor road must give way to traffic on a major road.

L – Look in all directions at the earliest point from which you can see. Keep looking as you slow down and stop — if necessary, until you are sure it is safe to turn.

Don't forget!

Take a "lifesaver" glance over your left shoulder just before you turn.

Turning right into a major road

- Assess the junction. Check road signs and markings.
- Use the OSM/PSL routine

O – Look in your mirrors and over your right shoulder to assess what's behind.

S – Signal right in good time.

M – Manoeuvre, use PSL

P – Position yourself as close to the centre of the road as is safe.

In a one-way street, position yourself on the right-hand side of the road.

When turning right, it is important to take up your position early.

S – Reduce speed. Be prepared to stop: you must give way to traffic on a major road.

L – Look in all directions at the earliest point from which you can see. Keep looking as you slow down and stop — if necessary, until you are sure it is safe to turn.

Don't forget!

Take a "Lifesaver" glance over your right shoulder just before you turn.

Fig. 11.4 Emerging to turn left or right

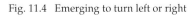

Turning right into a side road

Use the OSM routine on approach.

Road Position

- Position yourself as close to the centre of the road as is safe, so that vehicles can pass on your left.

- In a one-way street, keep to the right-hand side of the road.

Oncoming traffic

- Adjust your speed as necessary

- Watch out for approaching traffic. Stop if necessary.

- Watch particularly for vehicles overtaking oncoming traffic

Emerging vehicles

- Watch for vehicles waiting to emerge from side road.

Pedestrians

- Make sure pedestrians are clear of your path before you turn. They have priority

Turning

- Take the 'Lifesaver' glance over your right shoulder just before you turn.

- Don't cut the corner.

- Don't accelerate fiercely. Your engine should be just pulling as you turn.

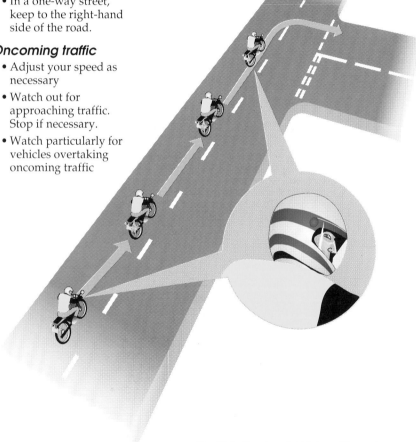

Fig. 11.5   Turning right into a side road

Turning left into a side road

Use the OSM routine on approach.

Road position

Your road position should be well to the left, about 3 feet from the kerb.

Speed

Left turns are often sharper than right turns, so reduce your speed accordingly.

Parked Vehicles

Look out for vehicles stopping to park before a left-hand junction, and also those parked immediately after the junction.

Pedestrians

Watch out for pedestrians who may be crossing when you turn. They have priority.

Cyclists

Keep a special lookout for cyclists coming up on your left.

Hazards

Take a 'Lifesaver' glance over your left shoulder just before you turn.

Take special care when

- Crossing a bicycle track or bus lane
- Pedestrians are crossing. They have priority
- The road surface is poor

After the turn

If it's safe to do so

- Speed up gradually as you leave the junction
- Remember to cancel your signal
- Check behind so you know what's following you

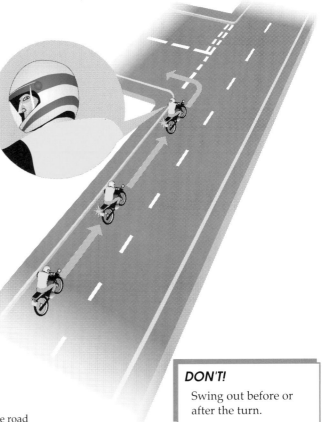

Fig. 11.6 Turning left into a side road

DON'T!
Swing out before or after the turn.

11. Riding in Traffic

Crossroads

Signs or road markings

The procedure when turning at crossroads is much the same as at any other junction.

You'll need to assess the crossroads on approach, so look well ahead and check for road signs and markings that might indicate priority.

Unmarked crossroads

Treat unmarked crossroads with extreme caution since neither road has priority.

Use the OSM-PSL routine.

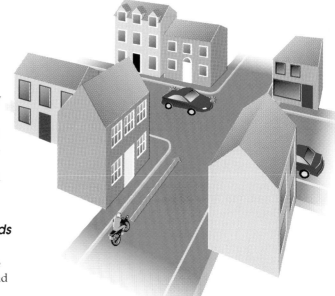

Fig. 11.7 Crossroads

When going ahead

Even if you have priority, look both ways for emerging traffic that might not have seen you.

Where the roads are narrow and vision restricted, you'll need to slow down as well. Be prepared to give way.

Turning traffic

Look out for vehicles turning right that might cross your path, particularly if you are also turning right.

Accident black spots

Crossroads are often accident black spots, so take extra care.

Fig. 11.8 Turning at crossroads

Passing side roads

Emerging vehicles

Look out for road signs indicating side roads, even if you are not turning off.

Often views are obscured at these junctions. A driver might pull out in front of you.

If you doubt that the driver has seen you, slow down and sound your horn. Be prepared to stop, if necessary.

Don't overtake at or approaching a side road.

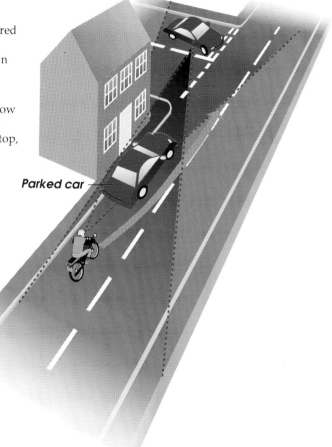

Parked car

Fig. 11.9   Restricted view of car emerging from side road

11. Riding in Traffic

Roundabouts

Roundabouts allow traffic from different roads to merge without necessarily stopping.

Procedure

- Before you enter a roundabout, give way to any traffic on your immediate right unless road markings indicate otherwise.
- Keep moving if the way is clear.

Going left

- Indicate left as you approach.
- Approach in the left-hand lane.
- Keep to that lane on the roundabout.
- Indicate left through the roundabout.

Going forward

- Approach in the left-hand lane without signalling. No signal is necessary. If you can't use the left-hand lane, for example, because it is blocked, use the next lane to it.
- Keep to that lane on the roundabout.
- Indicate left as you pass the exit just before the one you intend to take.

Going right

- Indicate right as you approach and maintain the signal on the roundabout.
- Approach in the right-hand lane.
- Keep to that lane on the roundabout.
- Indicate left as you pass the exit just before the one you intend to take.

Priority

Occasionally, traffic on the roundabout has to give way to traffic entering. Look-out for give-way lines on the roundabout.

Road surface

Like any junction, roundabouts are places where braking and acceleration occur. The road surface can become polished and slippery when wet.

DON'T!

Forget to take a 'Lifesaver' glance over your left shoulder to ensure it is safe to leave the roundabout.

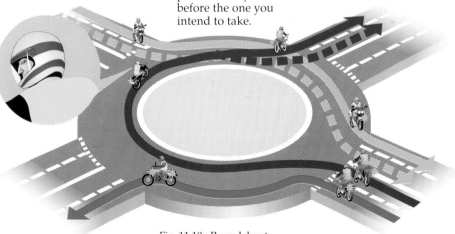

Fig. 11.10   Roundabout

Mini roundabouts

- Approach these in the same way as a roundabout. But remember, there's less space and time to signal and manoeuvre.

- Vehicles coming towards you might want to turn right. Give way to these.

- Be sure any vehicle on the roundabout is going to leave it before you join the roundabout.

- Beware of drivers who are using the roundabout for a U-turn.

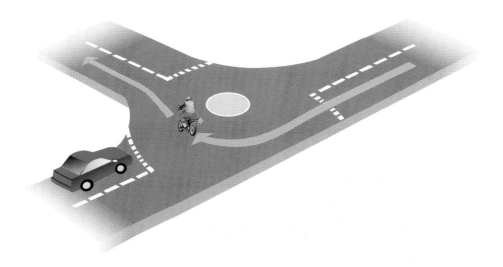

Fig. 11.11   Mini roundabout

Dual carriageways

Dual carriageways have at least two lanes in each direction, divided by a central reserve where there may be a safety barrier.

Caution

Some dual carriageways seem no different to motorways. However, motorway regulations do not apply.

Beware of slow-moving vehicles such as farm tractors.

Turning right from a dual carriageway

The central reserve sometimes has gaps for turning right. These may have special approach lanes.

To turn right, look behind, signal and move to the correct lane (OSM-PSL). Don't forget the 'Lifesaver' glance.

Take care when turning. You may have to cross the path of fast oncoming vehicles in two or more lanes. If in doubt, wait.

Turning left from a dual carriageway

If there is no deceleration lane or slip road

- Make sure you follow the OSM-PSL drill when you turn left
- Signal your intentions clearly and in good time
- Slow down in good time

Fig. 11.12   Turning right from a dual carriageway

Emerging onto a dual carriageway to turn right

- You'll need to cross the first carriageway before you can join the carriageway you want.
- **If the central reserve is wide enough,** you can wait there for a gap in the traffic on the second carriageway.
- **If the central reserve is too narrow,** don't begin to move across until the dual carriageway is clear in both directions.

DO!
Always look **both** ways when joining dual carriageways.

Fig. 11.13   Turning left from a dual carriageway

Emerging onto a dual carriageway to turn left

- **If there's no acceleration lane or slip road,** emerge as you would to turn left on a single carriageway main road. (See page 99)

- **If there is an acceleration lane or slip road,** emerge as you would to join a motorway.
  - Accelerate to a suitable speed in the acceleration lane

  - Wait for a gap in the traffic and move into the left-hand lane
  - Stay in the left-hand lane until you get used to the speed of the traffic in the other lanes

Overtaking

When you want to overtake, it's vital to wait for a safe and suitable moment.

DON'T overtake

- Unless it's necessary
- If your view ahead is blocked
- If other drivers might not be able to see you
- If there isn't enough room
- If the road narrows
- If you're approaching a junction
- If you're within the zig-zag area of a pedestrian crossing
- If there's a NO OVERTAKING sign (see Highway Code p.53)
- If you have to cross a double continuous white line, or where the line on your side of the road is continuous. See the Highway Code, rules 71 and 72.
- If there is 'Dead Ground' i.e. a dip in the road which might conceal an oncoming vehicle.

Procedure (OSM-PSL)

To overtake, you'll often need to use some or all of these steps several times before the right moment arrives.

For example

O – Look behind

S – Consider signalling

M – Adjust position to give you the best view ahead

P – Check your position. Can you see ahead?

S – Have you enough speed and acceleration to overtake?

L – Look! Is it clear to overtake or how fast is other traffic approaching?

If you're satisfied, apply the OSM routine again

O – Observe

S – Signal

M – Manoeuvre

Remember!

- Take a 'Lifesaver' glance just before you move out.
- Overtake as quickly as you can and don't cut in.
- Never automatically follow an overtaking vehicle. There might not be enough time for both of you to overtake at once.

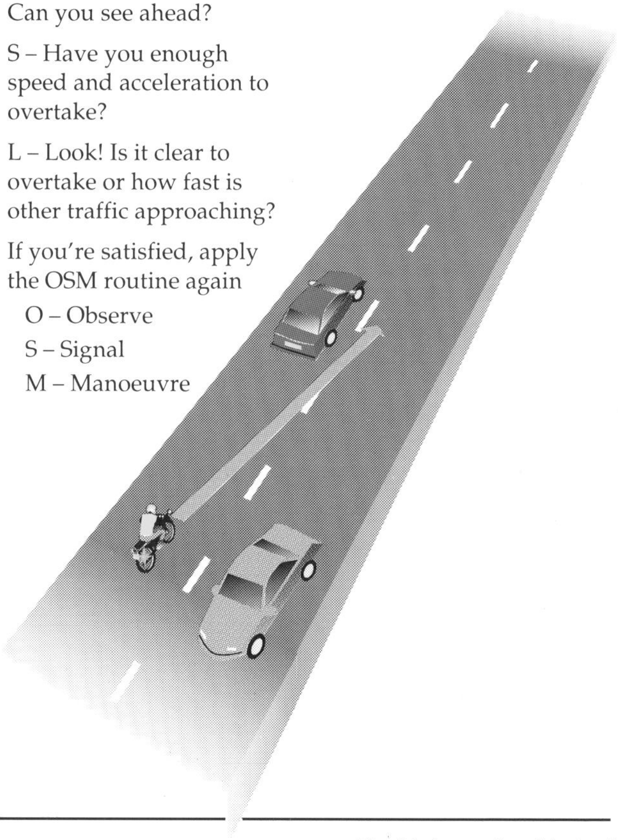

Fig. 11.14   Overtaking

Overtaking on the left

Overtake only on the right, except

- When the vehicle in front is signalling an intention to turn right, and you can overtake on the left without getting in the way of others
- You want to turn left at a junction
- Traffic is moving slowly in queues and vehicles in the lane on your right are moving more slowly than you are
- In a one-way street (but not on dual carriageways) where vehicles are allowed to pass on either side.

See Highway Code rule 88.

Judging speed and distance when overtaking

If you're travelling at 50mph and the oncoming vehicle is doing the same, you're approaching each other at 100mph or 150 feet per second.

So

- Give yourself plenty of time
- Take great care on a two-way, three lane road: a vehicle might pull out without warning while you're overtaking
- Try to get close enough to the vehicle in front of you to overtake safely, but not so close that you are unable to see the road ahead.

Keep a safe distance!

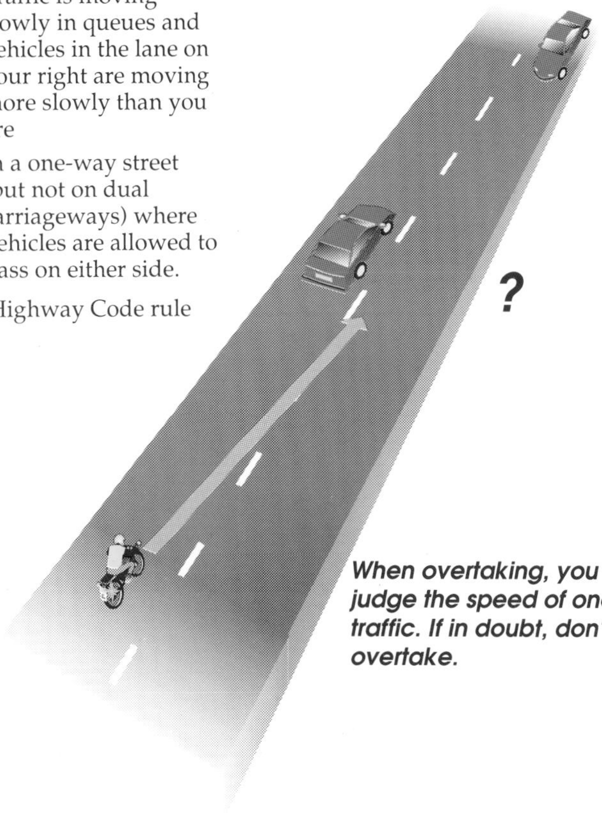

When overtaking, you must judge the speed of oncoming traffic. If in doubt, don't overtake.

Fig. 11.15 Overtaking: converging vehicles

11. Riding in Traffic

Overtaking on dual carriageways

Never overtake on the left unless you're travelling in queues of slow-moving traffic.

Don't overtake unless you are sure you can do so safely. Use the appropriate parts of the OSM/PSL procedure that are appropriate, for example

O – Look behind to assess the speed, course and position of following traffic.

P – Position yourself well back from the vehicle in front.

S – Speed: make sure you have enough in reserve to overtake.

L – Look ahead to make sure the lane you want to join is clear.

Use the OSM routine again.

M – Manoeuvre. Remember the 'Lifesaver' glance into the blind area before you change course. If you're satisfied that it's safe, overtake as quickly as you can and don't forget to cancel your signal.

Return to the left only when you're well clear of the vehicle you've overtaken. Don't cut in!

High speed riding

Remember, if you're travelling at high speed, it's safer to combine regular and sensible use of the mirrors with the 'Lifesaver' glance before you alter course. (See page 83)

Weaving

Don't weave from lane to lane.

Riding in the middle lane

Where there are three lanes, don't ride in the middle lane and so prevent drivers from overtaking you.

Riding in the left-hand lane

Use the left hand lane, unless the amount of slow moving traffic would cause you to continually move out to overtake.

Fig. 11.16 Overtaking on a dual carriageway

Motorways are different from ordinary roads as they are designed to help traffic travel faster more safely. This places greater demands on both rider and machine.

You must be the holder of a Full Motorcycle Licence (category A) if you want to ride on a motorway. Mopeds and small motorcycles (under 50cc) are not allowed on motorways at all.

High speed riding means that conditions can change rapidly, so you'll need to be alert, rested and feeling well. You'll need more time to stop, so leave a bigger gap between you and the vehicle in front.

Start your routines earlier when riding at high speeds.

12. Riding on Motorways

To ride on an motorway

You must

- Hold a Full Motorcycle Licence (learner riders are not allowed on motor-ways)
- Have a thorough knowledge of the sections of the Highway Code dealing with motorways
- Know and understand the special motorway warning signs and signals
- Have even greater concentration

Your motorcycle must be

- Of a suitable type for motorways (mopeds and some small motorcycles are not allowed on motor-ways).

- Maintained to a high standard. Pay particular attention to wheels, tyres and brakes.

You should also

- Plan your route
- Check that you have enough fuel for your journey

Don't attempt a long journey if you are tired or unwell.

High speeds demand greater concentration. If you're tired you won't react as quickly as you should.

Fig. 12.1 Motorway sign

Joining the motorway

- The slip road leads into an acceleration lane.

  Use this lane to increase your speed up to the speed of the traffic already on the motorway.

  Look for a gap in the traffic, and move out into the left-hand lane when it's safe.

- Stay in the left-hand lane until you are used to the speed of traffic in the other lanes.

  Remember!

  It takes time to get used to the speed of the other vehicles, so don't overtake immediately.

When other vehicles join

After passing an exit, there's usually an entry where other vehicles join. Don't try to race them! Reduce speed if necessary or, if it's safe, move out to the next lane.

Make sure you can see and be seen!

Always ride with dipped headlamp(s)!

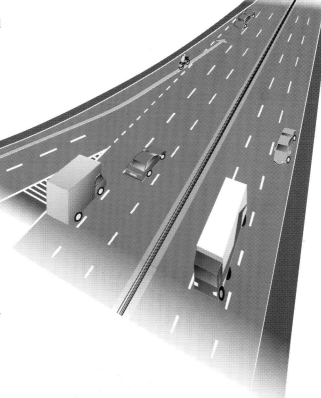

Fig. 12.2 Joining a motorway

12. Riding on Motorways

Road signs

Motorway signs tend to be much larger than ordinary road signs. This helps you to plan ahead because you can see them from further away.

Look out for flashing amber lights and signs indicating

- Lane closure
- Speed limits
- Roadworks
- Other hazards

Some signals have red lights as well. If the red lights flash above your lane, you must not go beyond the signal in that lane. If red lights flash on a slip road, you must not enter it.

Remember!

Flashing amber lights warn of danger ahead, so

- Use the OSM routine
- Slow down early.

Obstructions

If you find yourself catching up with slower moving traffic there could be an obstruction ahead. Keep well back! Be aware that other vehicles may slow down gradually without braking. You won't have warning from their brake lights.

Stopping on motorways

You must not stop on motorways unless

- It's an emergency
- You want to prevent an accident
- Police or road signs indicate you must

If you need to stop for a break, find a service area.

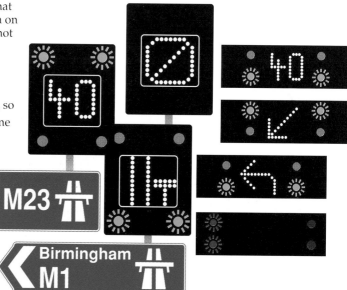

Fig. 12.3 Motorway signs to watch for

Where to stop

On the hard shoulder.

Remember! The hard shoulder is for emergency use only. It's not for parking or resting.

How to re-join the motorway from the hard shoulder

Don't pull straight out onto the main carriageway.

Use the hard shoulder as an acceleration lane to build up speed before joining the left-hand lane when there's a gap.

Leaving the motorway

- Move to the left-hand lane long before you intend to leave the motorway.
- Don't overtake when you're close to your exit.
- Move into the deceleration lane and slow down.
- Check your speedometer. Travelling fast for a long time can make you think you have slowed down more than you have.
- Some slip roads have sharp bends so slow down and approach these carefully.

Lane discipline

Keep in lane. Don't weave.

Change lane only if necessary. When you do change lanes, use the OSM routine much earlier than you would on ordinary roads. Give other drivers time to react.

Two-lane motorways

Use the left-hand lane for normal riding and the right-hand lane for overtaking only.

Three-lane motorways

Again, use the left-hand lane for normal riding. The middle and outside lane are for overtaking only. When the left-hand lane has a lot of slow-moving traffic, you can stay in the middle lane to avoid repeatedly moving in and out. Return to the left-hand lane after overtaking.

Remember!

The right hand lane is not for fast riding. It's for overtaking only.

Fig. 12.4   Leaving a motorway

12. Riding on Motorways

Overtaking

Never overtake on the left or use the hard shoulder. Always overtake on the right except in queues of slow-moving traffic.

Plan well ahead by using those parts of the OSM-PSL routine that are necessary in plenty of time. For instance

O – Use the mirrors to assess the speed, course, and position of following traffic.

P – Position yourself well back from the vehicle you intend to overtake.

S – Speed: make sure you have enough in reserve to be able to overtake.

L – Look ahead to ensure the lane you wish to join is clear.

O – Use the mirrors again to check the situation behind. Remember, traffic might be coming up from behind quicker than you think.

S – Signal early to give other drivers time to react.

M – Don't forget the 'Lifesaver' glance rearwards into the blind area before altering course. When it's safe, pull out into the overtaking lane and then cancel your signal.

Don't cut in! Allow plenty of room.

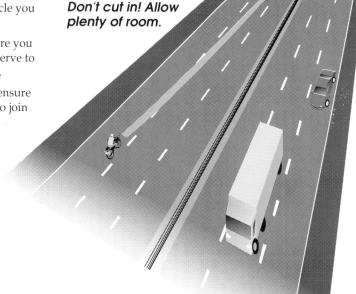

Fig. 12.5 Overtaking on a motorway

Because the weather in the British Isles is varied and uncertain, a serious motorcyclist must be prepared to ride in virtually all weathers.

The weather presents particular hazards for the rider, who must learn special techniques for safe riding.

The experienced rider is always prepared for the worst kind of weather for the time of year.

The experienced rider also knows when it is wiser not to ride.

13. Riding in Bad Weather

Wind

Strong cross-winds can make a motorcycle swerve. A cross-wind can hit you suddenly

- As you pass gateways on roads with high hedges
- As you come out from the shelter of a large vehicle when overtaking, or when being overtaken
- On exposed roads

Keep your speed low where there is a danger of such winds, so that you stay in control.

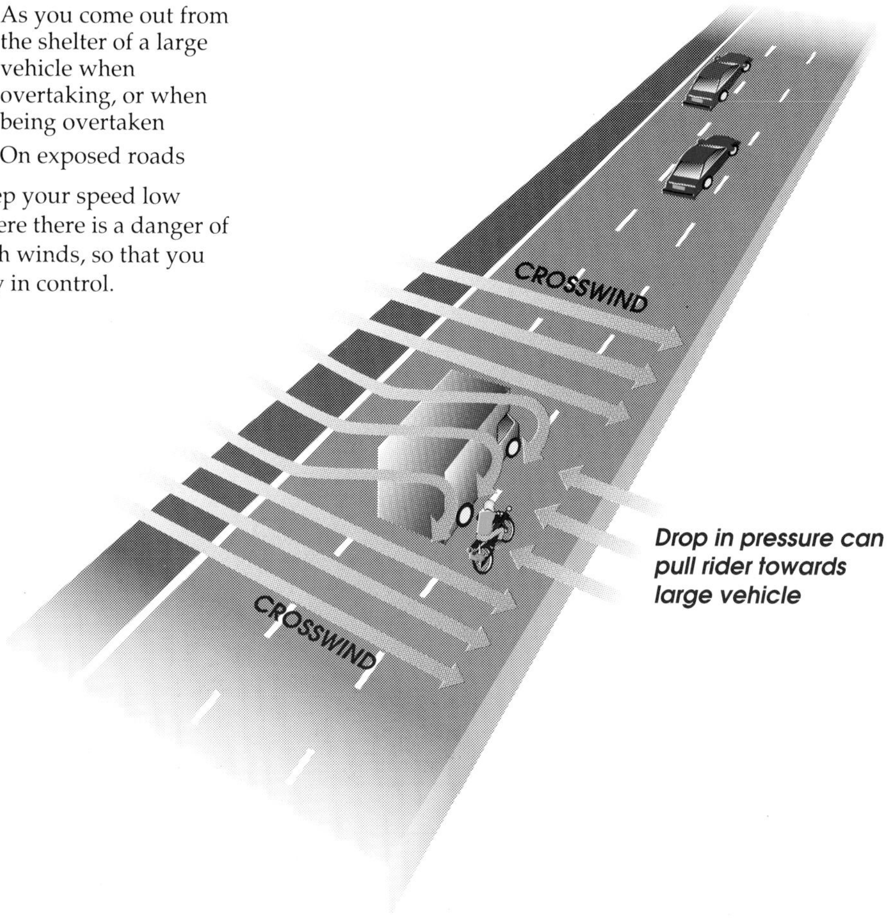

CROSSWIND

CROSSWIND

Drop in pressure can pull rider towards large vehicle

Fig. 13.1 Crosswind. Dangers when overtaking

Rain

Heavy rain on your visor or goggles can affect your view of the road. Slow down.

Consider others.

Try not to splash pedestrians by riding through pools of water on the road.

Fig. 13.2   Poor visibility in rain (through visor)

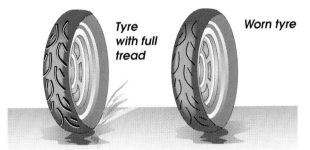

Tyre with full tread

Worn tyre

Worn tyres deal less effectively with surface water

Fig. 13.3   Surface water and tyre grip

Surface water

Keep your speed down in surface water or floods. Water can build up on your tyres in heavy rain and reduce their grip.

Water can suddenly cause your engine to stop, or affect

- Your balance
- The steering and brakes

Floods

If you have to ride through a flood,

1. Ride where the water is most shallow (usually at the crown of the road). Watch out for oncoming vehicles which may be doing the same.

2. Ride in low gear, and keep your engine running fast enough to keep water out of the exhaust system.

3. Test your brakes when riding slowly after you pass the flood, even if you have pushed your bike through the flood.

Fig. 13.4   Riding through a flood

13. Riding in Bad Weather

Mist and Fog

Mist and fog can arise suddenly, so be prepared.

Keep your distance from vehicles you are following, even though you may think they help you through the fog.

If they brake or stop suddenly, you may not be able to avoid an accident.

Fig. 13.5   Poor visibility in fog

Fig. 13.6   Effectiveness of rear foglamps

Coloured Cats Eyes

On motorways and some dual carriageways (see rule 116 of the Highway Code). They help in fog to find exits and entrances. The colours are

- Left edge of carriageway: red
- Right edge of carriageway: amber
- Acceleration/ deceleration lane: green
- Between lanes: white

Low visibility

Using headlamps

In weather which reduces visibility, you must switch on your lights. Keep all your lamps clear.

Rear fog lamps

When visibility drops below 100 metres, use your rear fog light, if your bike has one.

Speed in low visibility

Your speed in low visibility must allow you to stop safely within the distance you can see to be clear. That could mean slowing down when other drivers are not.

Position on the road

Keep away from the centre of the road markings. Approaching road users could also be driving near the centre.

Junctions

Be specially careful at junctions. You will be less able to see other traffic. On a motorcycle, it is also harder to hear it. If you can't see others, they can't see you.

Black Ice

Black ice is very dangerous. It happens when droplets of water freeze on a normally good, skid-resistant surface.

How to recognise black ice

If the road looks wet, but you can't hear tyre noise as you would on a wet road, suspect black ice.

Ice or Snow

It is often better to keep to main roads during ice and snow. These are more likely to be clear and well gritted.

Road markings

Snow hides road markings, so be careful. *You* might have local knowledge but *others* might not.

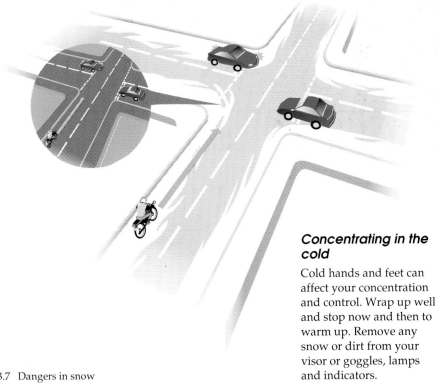

Fig. 13.7 Dangers in snow

Concentrating in the cold

Cold hands and feet can affect your concentration and control. Wrap up well and stop now and then to warm up. Remove any snow or dirt from your visor or goggles, lamps and indicators.

13. Riding in Bad Weather

Hot weather

Motorcycling is probably at its best during hot weather, but there can still be surface problems.

- Melted tar can reduce tyre grip
- Rubber and dust deposits mixed with a rain shower after a dry spell can make the surface very slippery.

Never ride
- *in shorts or trainers*
- *bare armed*

Always wear full protective clothing

Fig. 13.8 Don't dress dangerously in hot weather

Riding at night is another aspect of motorcycling which demands special techniques and precautions.

The problems of riding at night vary widely with the type of road and the amount of traffic, but this section deals with the most important aspects.

14. Riding at Night

The two main requirements for riding at night are seeing and being seen.

Seeing at night

- Have your eyesight checked by an optician if you have any doubt about your sight in the dark
- Keep your goggles or visor clean. Scratches on the lens can cause dazzle from approaching traffic

  Replace goggles or visor if a lens becomes scratched
- Make sure your headlamp is correctly adjusted
- Make sure you can find the switches in the dark

Fig. 14.1   Headlamps of oncoming traffic

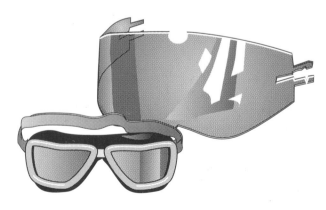

Fig. 14.2   Tinted visor and goggles

DON'T!
Wear tinted glasses, goggles or visors when riding at night or in poor daylight.

The Motorcycling Manual

Lamps

You must use dipped headlamp(s)

- When street lighting is poor, even when using your running lights
- In poor daylight
- On lighted motorways and other high-speed roads.

To help other road users to see you, ride with dipped headlamp(s) at all times — even in good daylight.

Fig. 14.3 Dipped beam

When you dip your headlamp(s)

- You will see less of the road ahead
- Slow down so you can stop within the distance you can see.

Use full headlamp(s)

- If there is no street lighting. Remember to dip for all road users: drivers, cyclists and pedestrians
- In any conditions when other traffic is using headlamps. Don't forget to dip.

Fig. 14.4 Main beam

DON'T

Use your main beam in the face of oncoming traffic. You could cause an accident.

Fig. 14.5 Use of dipped beam

If you're dazzled

- Don't retaliate. Keep your headlamp dipped.
- Slow down or even stop, if necessary.

14. Riding at Night

Being Seen

DO!

- Ride with dipped headlamps, unless you need to use the full beam.
- Wear reflective clothing. Fluorescent clothing will not show in the dark.
- Keep your reflective number-plate clean.
- Keep your lamps clean and in good working order. Carry a spare set of bulbs.

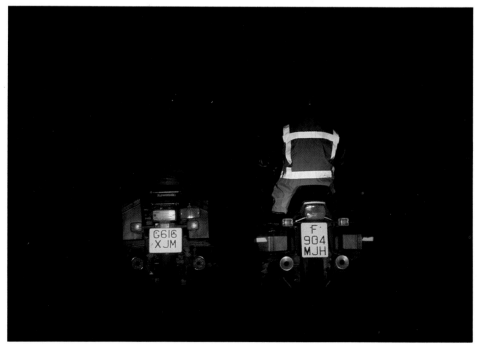

Fig. 14.6   Effectiveness of reflective clothing

Carrying a passenger puts extra responsibility on the motorcyclist.

Unless you have a Full Motorcycle Licence, you must not carry a pillion passenger or pull a trailer.

All riders are allowed to carry loads, including side panniers.

This section covers the problems and techniques of carrying passengers and loads.

15. Carrying a Passenger or a Load

Carrying a passenger

Licence

You're allowed to carry a pillion passenger, only if you've passed your motorcycle test and hold a Full Motorcycle Licence

The design of your motorcycle

You should only carry a pillion passenger if your motorcycle is designed to carry one.

To carry a passenger, your motorcycle should have

- Rear foot rests
- A proper passenger seat

Your passenger must

- Sit astride the bike facing forward. No side-saddling!
- Wear an approved motorcycle helmet properly fastened

The condition of your motorcycle

- Inflate the tyres according to the maker's instructions
- Adjust shock absorbers to allow for the extra weight

The passenger's clothing

Your passenger's clothing should be

- Protective
- Preferably bright and reflective

See Section 4.

Ride with extra care

Until you get used to carrying a passenger, particularly if your passenger has never ridden pillion before.

REMEMBER!

It is the rider's responsibility to

- Check behind
- Give signals
- Keep the motorcycle balanced

DON'T

Allow your passenger to wear loose items such as belts or scarves. These can become tangled in the wheel or driving chain and cause serious injury.

Instruct your passenger on how to ride safely

Some passengers might never have ridden pillion before. Ask them, if you don't know.

Instruct an inexperienced passenger to

- Keep both feet on the foot rests until dismounting.
- Lean with you while going round bends and corners
- Keep a light but firm hold on your waist or hip, or on the passenger grab handle, if fitted

Instruct your passenger not to

- Look behind
- Lean to the side to see ahead. This will affect your balance.

Fig. 15.1   Your passenger must wear the correct clothing

DON'T

- Ask your passenger to look behind or signal for you
- Accept any road or traffic information from your passenger, without verifying it
- Carry young children on a motorcycle

15. Carrying a Passenger or a Load

Carrying a load

Side panniers

Use side panniers or a top box to carry a load. These make sure the weight is properly secured.

Carrying a load on front

Don't carry a load on the front. It might affect your steering.

Tankbags are available and give extra carrying capacity.

Adjusting your motorcycle

Make any necessary adjustments to the

- Suspension
- Steering
- Tyres
- Lights

Ride carefully!

When riding with a load, ride very carefully until you are used to the 'feel' of the extra weight.

Fig. 15.2 Motorcycle with side panniers

Side-car outfits

If you want to fit a side-car

- Ask your dealer if your machine is suitable
- Make sure that, after fitting, the side-car is fixed correctly to the mounting points

Aligning the side-car

Make sure bike and side-car are correctly aligned. If they are not, the outfit will be difficult to control and probably dangerous.

Fig. 15.3 Sidecar outfit

15. Carrying a Passenger or a Load

Riding techniques

You must adapt your riding technique when riding a bike with a side-car. Keep your speed down until you've mastered it.

Bends and turning

On bends and when turning, the side-car outfit must be steered because the rider cannot lean the machine over. This requires a deliberate push or pull on the handlebar.

Approach corners at a suitable speed.

Even slight acceleration during a left turn may cause the side-car to lift off the road.

Stopping distances

Remember, the extra weight of the side-car will need a greater stopping distance.

Braking

Unless a brake is fitted to the side-car wheel, the outfit will tend to pull to the right, if you brake hard.

Sidecar outfits need special care on bends

Fig. 15.4   Problems cornering with sidecar outfit

A motorcycle needs routine attention and maintenance. Without this, it will soon get into a dangerous condition.

Many jobs need expert mechanical knowledge, but you can do simple routine maintenance yourself with the aid of the maker's handbook.

Rider training courses may include some mechanical instruction and advice on maintenance. You should learn how to do routine maintenance yourself.

If you haven't the skill to do the more difficult tasks, get a qualified person to do them.

16. Basic Maintenance

Regular checks
- Tyres
- Wheels
- Lights
- Indicators

And these controls
- Brakes
- Clutch
- Throttle controls

These should
- Operate smoothly
- Have no kinks in outer cables
- Have no fraying on the inner cable

Check fluid levels
- Engine oil
- Gearbox oil
- Distilled water in battery
- Radiator water, if your engine is water cooled
- Brake fluid if you have disc brakes

Check your exhaust system
It must be in good repair and not punctured or noisy.

Check your sparkplugs
Dirty plugs cause poor starting.

Learn how to
- Clean the plugs
- Check and set the gap

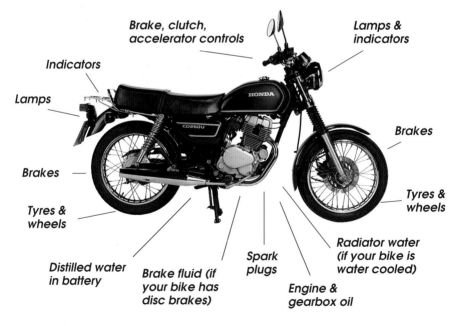

Brake, clutch, accelerator controls

Lamps & indicators

Indicators

Lamps

Brakes

Tyres & wheels

Brakes

Tyres & wheels

Distilled water in battery

Brake fluid (if your bike has disc brakes)

Spark plugs

Engine & gearbox oil

Radiator water (if your bike is water cooled)

Fig. 16.1   Parts you should check regularly

Brakes

Brake systems are either mechanical, hydraulic, or a combination of these.

Moving parts

The strain on brake cables and levers causes them to wear and so need lubrication.

Brake pads and shoes become less effective when worn. These items must be checked often and replaced from time to time.

Hydraulic brakes

If your bike has hydraulic brakes

- Check brake fluid level regularly
- Check couplings and joints for fluid leaks

Fig. 16.2 Items you'll need regularly

Drive chains

Drive chain wear

A loose or tight chain will cause wear on the driving chain and sprockets. If the driving sprocket is worn

- The chain won't be held in position
- The chain might slip off the sprocket and the rear wheel could lock.

Adjusting the drive chain

This is important. Make sure the connecting link is correctly fitted and secure. Chains stretch with wear and must be replaced.

Lubricating the drive chain

Lubricate the driving chain regularly with a suitable oil. See your manufacturer's handbook.

Fig. 16.3 Chain and links

Tyres

Tyre pressures

- Always keep each tyre at the pressure recommended in the maker's handbook
- Check pressures
  - at least weekly
  - before a trip, when the tyres are cold
- Use a reliable pressure gauge
- Don't vary the pressure to suit your own weight

  (You might have to increase the pressure when carrying a pillion passenger)
- Riding at a sustained high speed might require a higher pressure. See maker's handbook.

If there is any sign that the tube or tyre has been punctured, make sure it is permanently repaired.

Warning

Your tyres are vital to your safety. Do not ride if you suspect your tyres are below the legal limit.

The police hold spot checks, so be prepared.

Tyre condition

Check your tyres for

- Grease or oil remaining on them
- The correct amount of tread
- Small stones or glass lodged between the tread
- Uneven tread wear indicating an incorrectly balanced or poorly aligned wheel
- Cuts or bulges

Replace any defective or illegal tyres.

Fig. 16.4 Damaged tyres

16. Basic Maintenance

Tyre regulations

You must not use
ANY TYRE that

1. Has a cut
   - longer than 25mm, or 10% of the width of the tyre, whichever is the greater, and/or
   - deep enough to reach the ply
2. Has a lump, bulge or tear caused by the part failure of its structure
3. Has any exposed ply or cord
4. Has been recut

Fig. 16.5 Worn tyres

Minimum tyre tread

On any tyre

1. Tread grooves
   The base of any groove which showed in the original tread **must be clearly seen.**
2. If your motorcycle has an engine capacity of **more than 50cc.**

   a. Tread pattern

   The grooves on the tread pattern of **all tyres** must be not less than 1mm deep forming a continuous band at least **three quarters** of the breadth of the tread and all **the way around.**

   b. Depth of tread

   The entire original tread must be visible with a continuous band **all** of the way around.
3. If your motorcycle has an engine capacity of less than 50cc, the tread of the tyre may be less than 1mm **if** the tread pattern can be clearly seen over the whole tread area.

For further information see *How Safe is Your Motorcycle* (HMSO)

Punctures

To avoid getting a puncture, look out for sharp objects such as glass or metal on the road.

If a tyre hits a sharp object or a pothole, stop as soon as you can and check the tyre for damage.

A machine designed for the road should not be taken over uneven surfaces at high speed. This can damage tyres and wheels.

If your machine suddenly becomes unstable, a puncture might be the cause.

If this happens, or a tyre bursts,

- Don't brake suddenly
- Hold the handlebars firmly
- Close the throttle to make the machine slow down
- Try to keep a straight course
- Stop gradually at the side of the road

A punctured tyre should be properly repaired or replaced.

Replacing a tyre

- When replacing a tyre, be sure to buy the correct type. Some machines may require a different type of tyre on the front and back wheel.
- With tubed tyres, it's best to change the inner tube at the same time.
- When changing tyres, check inside the new tyre for sharp objects.
- The tread on new tyres tends to be rather shiny.

You won't get the full grip until this shininess wears off. This could take up to 100 miles.

So, ride with extra care with new tyres, especially on wet or slippery roads.

Wheels

Condition of wheels

Check that the wheels are running 'true'.

Spin each wheel in turn and watch it where the rim passes a suspension arm or mudguard stay. If the wheel is buckled this will show up. Check also for damaged spokes.

Do not ride with

- Damaged or missing spokes
- An out-of-line or buckled wheel

Have your wheels balanced regularly by an authorised dealer.

Cleaning your machine

Motorcycles should be cleaned regularly because they are much more exposed to road dirt than other vehicles.

Experienced riders know the importance of cleaning. It's much more than just wanting to ride a gleaming bike.

They know a clean machine will probably run better.

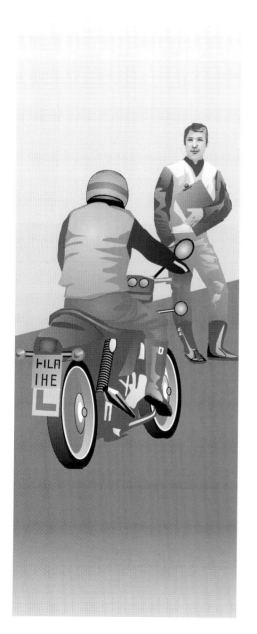

The regulations which govern motorcycle riding now call for Compulsory Basic Training to be taken before a you can apply for the Motorcycle Test (See Section 6).

The main requirements of the Motorcycle Test are the same as for the Driving Test. This section outlines the main features.

You can find full details of the Motorcycle Test, and the officially recommended syllabus for learning to ride, in the book *Your Driving Test* (HMSO), available in any good bookshop.

Your questions answered

Does the standard of the test vary?

No! All examiners are trained to carry out tests to the same standard.

Test routes

- Are as uniform as possible
- Include a range of typical road and traffic conditions

You should have the same result from different examiners or at different Driving Test Centres.

Are examiners supervised?

Yes! They are closely supervised. A senior officer may be present at your test.

Don't worry about this.

The senior officer won't be examining you, but making sure the examiner is testing you properly.

Since the senior officer will not interfere with the test or the result, just carry on as if he or she wasn't there.

How the examiner will test you

When you are taking the test, the examiner will follow you either on a motorcycle or in a car, except during the emergency stop exercise.

Your test will be carried out over a route covering a wide variety of traffic conditions.

Before the test you will be fitted with

- Earphones under your helmet
- A radio receiver on a waist belt

What will the examiner want from you?

The examiner will want to see you ride safely and competently under various road and traffic conditions.

He (or she) will

- Give you directions clearly and in good time
- Ask you to carry out set exercises

The examiner will be understanding and sympathetic, and will make every effort to put you at ease.

How should you ride during the test?

Ride in the way your instructor has taught you.

If you make a mistake, don't worry. It might be minor and may not affect your result.

The examiner will be looking for an overall safe ride.

What's the purpose of the test?

The motorcycle test is designed to see if

- You can ride safely
- You know and understand the Highway Code
- You understand other motorcycling matters, such as
  - what causes skids and how to control them
  - the importance of maintenance

The test ensures that all riders reach a minimum standard.

The motorcycle test is straightforward

You will pass if

You can satisfy the examiner that you can

- Ride safely
- Do the set exercises
- Show enough knowledge of the Highway Code

How long will the test last?

About 35 minutes.

What will the test include?

Apart from general riding which we will talk about later, your test will include

- An eyesight test
- Special exercises, such as
  - an emergency stop
  - turning in the road
- Questions on
  - the Highway Code
  - other motorcycling matters

What's the order of the test?

The eyesight test is first.

If you fail that, the test will not go ahead.

After the eyesight test, the order is up to the examiner.

What about the special exercises?

The first special exercise, usually the emergency stop, normally comes after a short ride.

The examiner will be as helpful as possible, and will

- Ask you to pull up at the left side of the road
- Explain any one of the special exercises and ask you to carry it out

Make sure you understand!

If you're not sure about anything, ask! The examiner will explain again.

The other special exercises will be spread over the test route.

When you've passed

You'll be allowed to ride

- Without L-plates
- Unsupervised
- On motorways

However, it takes lots of practice to become a really skilled rider. Further tuition is recommended.

The application form

- Ask for form DL26 at any Post Office or Driving Standards Agency Regional Office. You'll find the address in your local telephone directory or Yellow Pages.

If you wish to take the test in the Welsh language, please indicate this on the form.

- Complete the form, and send it with the appropriate fee to your Driving Standards Agency Regional Office.
- Apply well before the time you want to be tested.
- Give the earliest date you think you'll be ready.
- You should also include your Certificate of Completion of an Approved Training Course (CBT certificate: DL 196) or valid Part 1 Certificate.

If you don't send this with your application, you must show it to the examiner when you attend for your test.

If you fail to do so your test will not go ahead, and you'll lose your fee.

Special circumstances

To make sure that enough time is allowed for your test, it would help the DSA to know

- If you are profoundly deaf
- If you are restricted in any way in your movements
- If you have any disability which may affect your riding

If any of these apply to you, please write this on your application form.

If you can't speak English or are deaf, you are allowed to bring an interpreter.

Your test appointment

Your DSA Regional Office will send you an appointment card.

This will give you

- The time and date of your appointment
- The address of the Driving Test Centre
- Other important information.

Postponing your test appointment

Contact the DSA Regional Office where you booked your test if

- The date or time on the card is not suitable
- You want to postpone or cancel the test

You must give at least 10 clear working days notice, (that is, two weeks—longer if there is a bank holiday) not counting

- The day the Office received your request
- The day of the test

If you don't give enough notice, you will lose your fee.

Your driving licence

Make sure that you have your provisional driving licence with you, and that you have signed it.

If you don't, you'll need some other form of identity. Any of the following are acceptable

- A signed driving licence issued in

  - Great Britain, Northern Ireland, the Channel Islands, or the Isle of Man

  - an EC member state

  - a country whose driving licences can be exchanged for a United Kingdom Driving Licence

- A signed passport

- A signed International Driving Permit

- A signed British Forces Licence

- A signed identity card issued by your employer. This must show

  - your name written in roman letters (such as ordinary printing)

  - your photograph

  - your signature

Remember

It's up to you to satisfy the examiner. Otherwise, your test will be cancelled.

Your test motorcycle

Make sure that the motorcycle you intend to ride during your test is

- Legally roadworthy and has a current test certificate, if it is over the prescribed age

- Fully covered by insurance for its present use and for you to ride

- Properly licensed with the correct disc displayed

- Displaying L-plates where required, which are visible from the front and rear

If you overlook any of these

- Your test may be cancelled

- You could lose your fee

The eyesight test

What the test requires

You must satisfy the examiner that, in good daylight, you can read a vehicle number-plate with letters 79.4mm (3.1 inches) high

Minimum distance

20.5 metres (about 67 feet)

If you need glasses

or contact lenses, wear them.

Continue to wear them during the test and whenever you ride.

How the examiner will test you

Before you mount your motorcycle, the examiner will point to a vehicle and ask you to read the number-plate.

If you are unable to read the number-plate, the examiner will measure the exact distance and repeat the test.

If you fail the eyesight test

If you can't satisfy the examiner that your eyesight is up to the standard required

- You will have failed your motorcycle test
- Your test will go no further

If you need glasses or contact lenses to pass the eyesight test, you must always wear them when you ride.

Fig. 17.1

The Highway Code

You must

- Show knowledge of the Highway Code
- Obey the rules set out in it

Other motorcycling matters

You must also show knowledge of other motorcycling matters, including

- Matters not covered in the Highway Code, such as
  - tyre wear
  - motorcycle and road safety
  - basic maintenance
- Behaviour and road holding of motorcycles in bad weather
- Keeping balance while carrying passengers

You must show that you know the Highway Code and that you can apply it.

How the examiner will test you

At the end of the test, your examiner will ask you some questions on the Highway Code and on other motorcycling matters.

You must answer these to the examiner's satisfaction, although small errors may not cause you to fail.

You will also be asked to identify some traffic signs.

But remember!

Knowing is not enough.

You must demonstrate your knowledge as you ride.

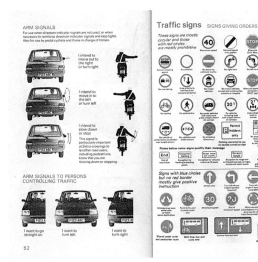

Fig. 17.2

17. The Motorcycle Test

Controlling your speed

What the test requires

You must make good progress along the road, bearing in mind

- Road conditions
- Traffic
- Weather
- Road signs and speed limits

How the examiner will test you

For this aspect of riding, there is no special exercise.

The examiner will watch carefully how you control your speed as you ride.

Skills you must master

You must

- Take great care in the use of speed
- Make sure you can stop safely, well within the distance you can see to be clear
- Leave a safe distance between yourself and other vehicles
- Leave extra distance on wet or slippery roads
- Ride at a steady speed within the speed limit

Faults you must avoid

- Riding too fast for the road or traffic conditions
- Changing your speed erratically

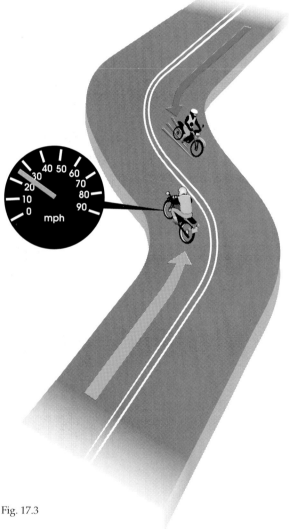

Fig. 17.3

Making progress

What the test requires

You must

- Make progress along the road
- Ride at a speed appropriate to road and traffic conditions
- Move off at junctions as soon as it is safe to do so

How the examiner will test you

For this aspect of riding, there is no special exercise.

The examiner will watch your riding, and will want to see you

- Making reasonable progress along the road
- Keeping up with traffic
- Showing confidence and sound judgement

Skills you must master

You must be able to

- Choose the correct speed for
  - the type of road
  - the type and density of traffic
  - the weather and visibility

- Approach all hazards at a safe speed without
  - being too cautious
  - interfering with the progress of other traffic

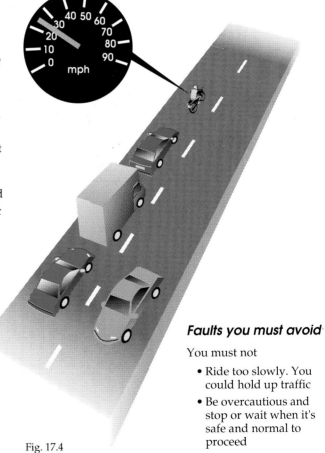

Fig. 17.4

Faults you must avoid

You must not

- Ride too slowly. You could hold up traffic
- Be overcautious and stop or wait when it's safe and normal to proceed

Awareness and anticipation

What the test requires

■ Awareness

You must

- Be aware of other road users at all times

■ Anticipation

You should try always to think ahead and plan ahead, and to

- Judge what other road users are going to do
- Predict how their actions would affect you
- React safely and in good time

What the examiner wants to see

You must show

- Awareness of and consideration for all road users, and
- Anticipation of possible danger and concern for safety

For example

■ Pedestrians

- Give way to pedestrians when turning from one road into another
- Take particular care with the very young, the disabled, and the elderly. They may not have seen you and could step out suddenly

■ Cyclists

- When crossing bus or cycle lanes, take special care
- Take special care with children cycling

■ Animals

- Take special care with people in charge of animals, especially horse riders

Faults you must avoid

- Repeatedly reacting suddenly to road or traffic conditions rather than anticipating them
- Showing irritation with other road users, particularly cyclists or pedestrians
- Sounding your horn aggressively
- 'Revving' your engine or edging forward when waiting for pedestrians to cross

Fig. 17.5

Special exercises

Braking

You must be able to combine the use of front and rear brakes correctly, in all weather conditions.

Make sure you fully understand the braking techniques explained by your instructor, and when to use them.

Emergency Stop

- Apply the front brake just before the rear
- Apply both brakes effectively
- Stop the machine as quickly as possible without locking either wheel

U-Turn

After the emergency stop exercise the examiner will ask you to ride in a U-turn and stop on the other side of the road.

Slow Ride

You will be asked to ride as in slow-moving traffic for a short distance, if the examiner has not already seen you doing this in queuing traffic.

Rear Observation

Even if you have mirrors fitted to your motorcycle, look over the appropriate shoulder to check the position of traffic before you

- Signal
- Change direction
- Slow down or stop

Take note of what you see and act on it.

Just looking is not enough!

Fig. 17.6

Index

Index

Index

U

V

W

Z